Family
BY THE
BIBLE™

CREATING, LEADING, AND MANAGING
HIGH-PERFORMANCE FAMILIES

David J. Sumanth, Ph.D.

WESTBOW
PRESS®
A DIVISION OF THOMAS NELSON
& ZONDERVAN

WestBow Press books may be ordered through booksellers or by contacting:

WestBow Press
A Division of Thomas Nelson & Zondervan
1663 Liberty Drive
Bloomington, IN 47403
www.westbowpress.com
844-714-3454

ISBN: 979-8-3850-1420-0 (sc)
ISBN: 979-8-3850-1421-7 (hc)
ISBN: 979-8-3850-1422-4 (e)

Library of Congress Control Number: 2023924153

Print information available on the last page.

WestBow Press rev. date: 01/25/2024

CONTENTS

To the memory of Paul J. Sumanth—Chaya's and my youngest son, and John's only brother—called home by God, on June 23, 2000, when he was just twenty years old. I also dedicate this work to my late mother, Nancy, for being my influencing mother; my beloved wife, Chaya, for being my devoted wife; my eldest son, John, for being my admiration; my daughter-in-law, Jaya, for her caring attention; our two "grands"—Miah and Anna, for the joy they bring to my heart; and my sister, Vivian, who has been my constant counselor for seventy-seven years.

SPECIAL NOTE

Most of the royalties from this book's sales will go to support the Paul J. Ministries, Inc. (www.pjsm.org)—a nonprofit, tax-exempt, 501c (3) organization, registered in Florida, and cofounded by Chaya and David Sumanth in 2001. PJSM has been supporting orphanages, churches, and schools in three countries since its inception, and aims to do so on a larger scale throughout the world because the needs of destitute children, youth, and adults are very compelling. According to the United Nations, each day, twenty-five thousand people, including more than ten thousand children, die from hunger and hunger-related causes. Some 854 million people worldwide are estimated to be undernourished.

We started the ministry with just one rented building in India, and twenty-two years later, we have three major hubs of ministry with fifteen campuses. We, with our partners, have graduated more than twenty thousand children from the tenth grade, in mostly English-medium schools. All glory and honor go to God, and much credit goes to our three directors and their wives: Suman and Manju Christopher; Jaideep and Sylvia Mukherjee; and Pastor Prakash and Priscilla Victor.

ACKNOWLEDGMENTS

My holy, living God receives all my praise. May His name be exalted—and may He receive all the glory and honor. Without His grace, leading, inspiration, faithfulness, and instruction, this book would never have been possible. I thank Him for giving me His inspired Word, the time-tested Torah, and the Holy Bible, full of God's proven wisdom of more than three millennia.

This book grew out of my keen observations of tens of thousands of families during the past seven decades. It's full of insights I learned from these many families, and I owe my deep gratitude to all of them for enabling me to reflect on and learn about their real concerns, questions, insights, and solutions. Many personal postulates about families have been filtered through the rich knowledge and wisdom of these tens of thousands—a powerful validation, in a way.

Many people have reviewed the manuscript and made invaluable suggestions; this book would not be in its present form without their wisdom, knowledge, and experience in dealing with families and their knowledge of the Bible. My deep appreciation goes to all of them. Finally, my special thanks are due to the editorial staff (Eric Shroedor, Eric Swanson, and others who were instrumental in making the book editing, design and production, and marketing possible.) at WestBow Press.

Chaya, my bride of forty-nine years, gets the credit for her constant encouragement and prodding to complete this book despite a major family tragedy and my two major illnesses. She typed most of this manuscript. Our eldest son, John's, charming wife, Jaya, also did some of the initial typing.

—David J. Sumanth, PhD

GETTING THE MOST OUT OF THIS BOOK

This book has been in the making for twenty years. It is written with seventy-four years of being a student of the Bible (from age three) and a practicing believer for sixty-one years after I began to follow Jesus' teachings at age sixteen. I have been teaching the Bible for sixty-one years. I have been a husband for forty-nine years, a father for forty-eight years, and a grandfather for fifteen years. My generational insights cut across many common issues for families. My cultural observations in more than one hundred countries also help make this work relevant and universal in scope and nature.

If your religious faith does not make you comfortable with the word *Bible*, it's best to read this book without being biased by its title. God's wisdom and real people's experiences are intertwined throughout this work.

This book can be read in sequence (recommended) or by topics of immediate need (if in a hurry). For example, if you are urgently interested in getting some ideas to better manage your finances, you could go straight to chapter 8. If you are interested in managing your time more productively, you may refer to chapter 9.

Knowledge of the Bible is not necessary to read, understand, and apply the concepts and principles of this book. It's written intentionally in an easy-to-understand tone.

Scripture references are embedded within the text for anyone to gain additional understanding or insights. Unless otherwise indicated, scripture is taken from the New King James Version.

OTHER PUBLICATIONS BY THE AUTHOR

Total Productivity Model: User's Manual, coauthor, A& M Printing, Inc., Chicago 1981.

The PQT Approach to Problem Solving: Volumes I and II, 1981, 1993, 2019.

Productivity Engineering and Management, McGraw Hill, NY, 1984.

Instructor's Manual to Accompany Productivity Engineering and Management, McGraw Hill, NY, 1984.

Productivity Engineering and Management, McGraw Hill, Singapore, 1985 (International Student Edition).

Productivity Management Frontiers I, editor, Elsevier Science Publishers B.V., The Netherlands, 1987.

Productivity Management Frontiers II, coeditor, Inderscience Enterprises Ltd., 1989.

Productivity Engineering and Management, Tata McGraw Hill, New Delhi, 1990.

Productivity and Quality Management Frontiers III, coeditor, Industrial Engineering and Management Press, Norcross, 1991.

Productivity and Quality Management Frontiers IV, volumes I– II, coeditor, Industrial Engineering and Management Press, Norcross, 1993.

Productivity Engineering and Management, Tata McGraw Hill, Primis Custom Publishing, 1994.

Ingenieria y Administracion de la Productividad, McGraw Hill, Mexico 1994 (Spanish Edition).

Productivity and Quality Management Frontiers V, coeditor, Industrial Engineering and Management Press, Norcross, 1995.

Customer Delight Management (CDM): A Necessary Approach for Survival into the 21ˢᵗ Century, 1995.

Productivity Measurement Guide: A Practical Approach for Productivity Measurement in Organizations, coauthor, McGraw-Hill, NY., 1996.

Productivity and Quality Management Frontiers VI, coeditor, Engineering and Management Press, Norcross, 1997.

Planning for Success, 1997.

Productivity and Quality Management Frontiers VII, coeditor, Engineering and Management Press, Norcross, 1998

Total Productivity Management, CRC Press, Boca Raton/Taylor and Francis, 1998.

Total Productivity Management, CRC Press, Boca Raton, 1999 (Indonesian Translation).

Administracion para la Productividad Total, CRC Press LLC, 1999.

Compania Editorial Continental, S.A. DE CV, 1999.

Grupo Patria Cultural, S.A. DE CV, 2000.

Productivity and Quality Management Frontiers VIII, coeditor, MCB University Press, England, 1999.

Productivity and Quality Management Frontiers IX, coeditor, Technion, Israel, 2000.

Productivity and Quality Management Frontiers X, coeditor, International Society for Productivity and Quality Research (ISPQR), Miami, 2004.

A 30-day Christian Devotional, 2005, 2017.

Productivity and Quality: A Multidisciplinary Perspective, coeditor, McGraw-Hill, New Delhi, 2006.

Administracion de la Productividad Eclesiastico: Los Principios, 2012 (exploring traditional and hybrid publishers).

Technology and Innovation Management (exploring traditional and hybrid publishers).

Productivity Management Principles for Pastors, Evangelists, and Lay Leaders, 2003–2023 (exploring traditional and hybrid publishers).

Chapter One
FAMILY: THE BASIC BUILDING BLOCK

Be fruitful, and multiply; fill the earth.
—GENESIS 1:28

Why This Book?

The family is the most fundamental unit of society and the oldest human institution and organization in history, yet we understand family less than language, science, medicine, art, business, management, leadership, engineering, and law. In the United States, we have been buried in social costs of hundreds of billions of dollars because of not realizing that prevention is better than a cure. Instead of addressing the root causes of these social costs, we have been trying to tackle the symptoms.

Why must you read this book and pay attention to what it says? The four most important reasons are authenticity, believability, credibility, and "doability."

Authenticity

Today, more than ever, people are looking for authenticity and not facades. I have written my views caringly and candidly. I have illustrated important truths and principles by using a few of my own stories of the last seventy-four years (I remember my past all the way back to my third year—well, now you know my age.). I have been transparent and vulnerable so that we can face family issues with empathy and without being preachy or insensitive. I will let you draw your own conclusions and apply your God-given wisdom to discern and apply the concepts and principles of this book.

Believability

All anecdotes and stories presented in this book are *real*—with real people in real situations. Thus, this is a book about everyday people like you and me and billions of others around the world. I have used many examples from many families, past and present, to reinforce the truths that I've learned from the past while looking to the future. Whenever a prescription or suggestion is made, I have made sure that it has been implemented with consistent success (most of the time) because people believe when something is real and not misleading.

Credibility

My mother and father taught me that integrity is one of the most important traits a human being can have. They reminded me all through my life that "a good name is better than great riches" (Proverbs 22:1). In my fifty years of university-level teaching in the United States and sixty-one years of Sunday Bible study teaching, I have tried hard to practice what I preach, although I have faltered many times, perhaps like you. When I have faltered, I have admitted it to God and to those who were affected by my decisions. This book presents a balanced perspective while pointing out the positive and negative aspects of life as relevant to a particular discussion about family dynamics.

Doability

This book is written from a practical standpoint so you can understand and apply its content. After all, we remember 95 percent of what we apply, 10 percent of what we hear, and 20 percent of what we hear and read. The theories behind this book's content have been tested and proven.

This book is doable and not merely readable. It is diagnostic as well as prescriptive. It does not simply point out issues or problems; it offers practical tips, insights, procedures, methods, and solutions to change for the better.

In a way, this book represents the collective wisdom of thousands of people from all walks of life and six generations of practical wisdom from six continents—from a public toilet cleaner to a president, from a child to a great-grandparent, from a Chinese person to an American, from a Christian to a Hindu, from a novice to a veteran, from a student to a teacher, and from an uneducated person to an intellectual heavyweight.

This book's title, *By the Bible*, is used for five practical reasons:

1. The Bible is the best-selling book of all time. Five billion copies have been sold. It was released in the first century AD/CE in Hebrew/Aramaic. That's almost two thousand years ago. When we hear about a *New York Times* bestseller, we rush to get it because we realize there's something *valuable* in that book.

I wonder how many of us really know that the Bible has sold more copies and been available longer than any other book. There's significant value in it. I was curious about the Bible and what it had to say. After reading it multiple times, I was awestruck. I discovered that it has presented truths to humans over a span of several hundred decades—with major implications for individuals and families.

2. The Bible is *practical* and *relevant* to our time. What's so great about the Bible? Well, it has covered any life topic you could ever imagine—from human emotions to human aspirations; jealousy to murder, rape, and incest; prostitutes to princes; work ethic to success; shipbuilding to high-rise buildings; channels in the seas to galaxies in outer space; enterprises to empires; and architecture to engineering, just to cite a few.

How could there be such a breadth and depth of coverage about life in just *one* book? How can a book still be so relevant after thousands of years? Every family issue facing us today in *every* part of the world is addressed in the Bible. Every truth stated in the Bible is time-tested. The Bible is practical. Many judicial systems in the United States and Europe are direct adaptations of the laws of Moses in the Bible. Did you know that today's shipbuilding industry borrowed many technical specifications from Noah's ark?

3. The Bible has been influential in world history. Martin Seymour-Smith's *The 100 Most Influential Books Ever Written*, lists both the Old Testament and the New Testament of the Bible. To capture the influence of the Bible would require thousands of pages. It has influenced people of all backgrounds, beliefs, positions, and interests.

Handel's *Messiah* is a great choral piece—and a compilation of the Bible verses set to wonderful music. The English agnostic and scientist Thomas Huxley admitted, "Throughout the history of the Western world, the scriptures have been the greatest instigators of revolt against the worst forms of tyranny." Abraham Lincoln, one of the most respected US presidents, claimed that reading the Bible was "the best cure for the blues." Shakespeare, in *The Merchant of Venice*, said, "The devil can cite scripture for his purpose." Robert E. Lee, the Confederate general, was influenced by the Bible so much so that he said, "In all my perplexities and distresses, the Bible has never failed to give me light and strength." Cecil B. DeMille, the famous director of *The Ten Commandments*, clearly saw the great influence the Bible has on human beings. He observed profoundly, "The greatest source of material for motion pictures is the Bible, and almost any chapter would serve as a basic idea for a motion picture." It's no wonder *The Passion of Christ*, was such a big hit when Mel Gibson, the actor and director, released it in 2004. The famous *Chosen* series (2021), featuring Jesus and His disciples, and directed by Dallas Jenkins, has a viewership of more than four hundred million as of 2023.

4. The ultimate theme of the Bible is love. In the 31,173 verses of the thirty-nine OT books and the twenty-seven NT books, the Bible has one important truth: God *loves every* human being so much that He even offered his own Son, Jesus Christ, to redeem us to Himself when we accept this fact by grace through faith (Ephesians 2:8–9).

Having been born in India, an ancient land of mystery and mysticism, I grew up among people of many languages, social customs, colors, religious faiths, and castes. It was such a diversified setting that I didn't even know what racism was until I traveled out of India for the first time in 1971. When I introduced my friends in India, I did so by their names and not by their skin color or ethnicity. My childhood friends—many of them still living today, and all of them still my friends—are Hindus, Muslims, and Christians. They speak Hindi, Telugu, Urdu, Marathi, Gujarati, Malayali, Tamil, Bengali, Kannada, Sindhi, Punjabi, Marwari, and several other languages.

From my youth, I believed that what the Bible says is *always* true and, therefore, that I must learn and apply its precepts. The God of the Bible I have known for seventy-four years is holy. He never lies, and He is trustworthy and loving. Therefore, I did not accept the prevalent thinking that not everyone is necessarily intelligent, that most people are lazy and don't mind being failures, and that we first must look out for ourselves. These concepts are the opposite of what the Bible teaches.

I worked full-time as a process engineer, industrial engineer, and manager of various operational areas of an Indian megacorporation of seventy-five thousand employees from 1969 until 1975. I took the Bible literally when it came to what it taught me: that I should deeply care for my fellow humans and love them as I love myself. In those six years, I never laid off, suspended, or fired an employee. I've been teaching at the university level for fifty years and am considered a caring but tough professor (my nickname on campus is "caring taskmaster"). I have never failed a student. I have always thought that I should take God seriously in what He says. Jesus summarized the Ten Commandments (Matthew 22:37–39; Mark 12:30–31; Deuteronomy 6:4–5) into two commandments:

1. Love (agape) the Lord, your God, with all your heart, soul, and mind.
2. Love (agape) your neighbor as yourself.

Here, *agape* is the Greek word for sacrificial love. The neighbor is not literally your neighbor; it is *anyone* who is in need.

If I obey concept 1, I must accept that God created every human being in His image (Genesis 1:27). I internalized this concept during all my university teaching years; I cannot accept the premise that people can be failures. People have been failures because society— parents, professors, employers, and managers—often set them up for failure and not for success.

If I obey the concept 2, then, as a professor, I must set up my students for success—from day one. I go over my clear expectations with my students on the first day. I spend a minimum of ten hours of class preparation per lecture hour to bring complex concepts to simple explanations. I create a disciplined, high-performance-seeking classroom environment, and students are encouraged and positively reinforced to excel. They are never ridiculed, and I emphasize to them regularly that *failure is not an option*. Having taught nearly ten thousand students in two American universities since 1973, I have never failed a student—by obeying the above commandments of Jesus.

Today, in affluent societies, it has become difficult to see or experience genuine, unselfish, and caring love from people. People are being treated like disposable assets in many corporations. They're being used for profit gains and not for people gains. Agape love is the glue that binds together individuals in families, families in communities, communities in countries, and countries in the world.

5. The Bible talks about the family comprehensively. A family is a highly complex social entity that teaches so many lessons about almost every single topic—from responsibility to rewards; tragedies to triumphs; jealousy to magnanimity; anxiety to calmness; failures to success; centralized authority to decentralized autonomy; romance to marriage to sex, friendships to fights; respecting authority to releasing anger, and so on. You get the picture. The greatest thing about the Bible is that it addresses everyone and more about all these matters.

The Bible has addressed the issues of families for more than 3,500 years. We have documented evidence of family issues tested time and again; why not capture the longitudinal wisdom of the Bible? Well, that's what I have done in this book. I have distilled the essence of the Bible's age-old wisdom and applied it to the family in all its facets. The result is this book.

As with any work, this one is no exception. It is a huge opportunity to improve its substance and style with feedback—perhaps from you. All feedback is appreciated.

Importance of the Family: Some Shocking Statistics.

The subject of family is covered in several academic disciplines, including psychology, sociology, psychiatry, anthropology, genetics, neurosciences, history, liberal arts, law, and medicine. However, the challenge has been a lack of an *integrated* approach to management of families in a *systemic*, cohesive, and practical manner—for the benefit of everyone.

It is disappointing to think that most of us have never studied family as a formal subject or course in our schools, colleges, or universities. Few, if any, have learned about the intricacies and complexities of marriage. Most of us continue to learn about marriage as we go along in life, but it's mostly the hard way. Those of us married for long have understood the difference between the significance of the wedding and the marriage. A wedding is a one-day euphoric event, but marriage is a long, arduous, patient, continuous improvement journey. A wedding involves romantic love, but marriage is a commitment to the agape or sacrificial love.

I believe there is much to learn about family. If we have not been taught about such an important subject in a systematic and formal manner, how can we create—let alone nurture and sustain—healthy, productive, and successful families in physical, emotional, and spiritual ways?

A lack of systemic understanding and teaching about family has resulted in several family dysfunctions: arguments and fights over money, communication, chores, children's proms and dating, curfew times, vacations, in-laws, poor performances in schools, colleges, universities, and workplaces; loss of family unity, resulting in separations and divorces; physical, emotional, and sexual abuse, including incest, teenage pregnancies, and abortions; children's abandonment, suicides, and homicides; and on and on. I humbly submit to you that the root cause of what we're witnessing worldwide is a spiritual problem.

The breakdown of family as a basic unit of the society has also resulted in several other strategic social costs associated with drug addiction, depression, loneliness, homelessness, juvenile delinquencies, robberies, rape, murder, low marriage rates, and low birth rates.

For fifty years, our educational systems have been diluting intellectual rigor, especially in technical disciplines. India is producing more engineers than the economic giant, the United States, which is outsourcing hundreds and thousands of jobs to India and China—two economies to watch out for in this century. Our global competitive potential has been diminishing ever since the oil embargo of 1973—first, with the advent of fuel-efficient (but high-quality) Japanese Toyotas, Nissans, Hondas, Mazdas, and Subarus, and next with the takeover of the consumer electronics industry. GE, RCA, and Zenith are no longer the leaders; instead, it is Sony, Toshiba, Sharp, and Samsung. Even the film giant, Columbia Pictures, a pure American icon of Hollywood, is owned today by Sony, a Japanese company.

Until 1973, the United States had no competition. It was virtually a monopoly. Since then, we have reached a stage where the number one automotive company in the world is not General Motors; it is Toyota. The number one consumer electronics company is not General Electric; it is Samsung. The longest life spans for people are not in the United States; they are in Japan.

Now, let's look at some staggering statistics about families (table 1.1).

Table 1.1. Staggering Statistics about Families in the USA

Source: U.S. Dept. of Commerce (USA.gov)

Population Estimates, July 1, 2022	333,287,557
Population, Census, April 1, 2020	331,449,281
Population, Census, April 1, 2010	308,745,538
Population per square mile, 2020	93.8
Persons, under 5 years	5.7%
Persons under 18 years	22.2%
Persons 65 years and over	16.8%
Female Persons	50.5%
Owner-occupied housing unit rate, 2017-21	64.6%
Households, 2017-21	124,010,992
Persons per household, 2017-21	2.6
Households with a computer, 2017-21	93.1%
High School graduate or higher, persons age 25+ years, 2017-21	88.9%
Bachelor's degree or higher, persons age 25+ years, 2017-21	33.7%
Median household income (in 2021 dollars), 2017-21	$69,021
Per capita income in past 12 months (in 2021 dollars), 2017-21	$37,638
Persons in poverty	11.6%
Total Employer establishments, 2020	8,000,178
Total Non-employer establishments, 2019	27,104,006
Total Employment, 2020	134,163,349

These statistics do not look great. We need to do many things, but most importantly, we must address the root causes and not the symptoms. The root causes can be traced to the family unit, which is in major disarray, turmoil, and dysfunction. No other advanced country in the world has a higher divorce rate than the United States. Only Sweden has a 0.1 percent greater divorce rate. The United States cannot be strong economically, politically, and morally unless it addresses the root issue: broken-down families. We need to address the issue candidly yet thoughtfully, reflectively but pragmatically, and in a simple yet systemic manner.

What about other countries when it comes to families? The United States accounts for 4.25 percent of the world's population (third in the world, after India and China) of 195 countries in 2023 (worldometers.info). The US contributes to 15.69 percent (the largest) of the world's economy (statistics.com), but it has one of the highest divorce rates in the world. Therefore, if such a powerful country has problems with the family unit and is trying to improve, I assume that the other 194 countries can learn something from it in economic and technological matters.

For nearly thirty-five years, I have been studying what I call the "technology gradient." The TG is the technology gap between one country and another in both the level and the rate of change (Sumanth, D. J. and Sumanth, J. J., 1988). Since the late 1990s, with the common use of the internet, TGs are flattening between very advanced countries and developing economies, thereby shrinking the competitive advantages of the former. Every country in the world is affected by what happens in the United States—for better or worse.

The TG has been reversed in some cases, including between the US and China in super-fast train technology and between the US and India in software engineering and information technology (IT). IT and social media have dramatically altered social, moral, and personal norms and behaviors during the past decade. Good cultural values, shaped for centuries and millennia, have been destroyed in just a few decades. Since families are the most basic units in each country, cultural values have deteriorated at the family unit level with distorting and disfiguring proven family values, starting with children shooting classmates and teachers.

We can't even imagine the influence of the latest artificial intelligence (AI) without any national norms for the behaviors of AI robots which, without restraint, can challenge our existential stability. For the first time in the history of humankind, digital technologies are becoming more competent than human brains. It's just a matter of a few years before our brains will be linked to sophisticated computer brains. As technologies become more complex, our families will be challenged to monitor the moral values our children and grandchildren will acquire and practice.

Does the Family Really Matter Today?

What seems important in people's lives can be best gleaned from a look at magazines in bookstores. While sports, beauty, autos, food, entertainment, and business sections stack several dozens of magazines, the family section, if one exists, has just a handful. Clearly, the market doesn't seem to recognize the need for substantially more material than this. There are hundreds of millions of family units in the world, and it doesn't take a genius to figure out that it would be important to devote more magazines to the topics and issues related to families.

During the fifty years I have lived in the United States, we have moved away from family values, family togetherness, and family friendliness. We've been hoping to rediscover the good old truths, values, and principles of families. Societies are only as strong as their fundamental units, and families are only as strong as their individual members. Doesn't it make sense to return to the foundations of families and build stronger societies in the world?

The family matters today for many reasons:

1. Smoothly functioning families create *effective* communities, which do the right things for themselves and for their countries.

2. Wholesome family units reduce the *social costs* related to drug abuse, loneliness, suicide, alcoholism, divorce, depression, and other emotional and spiritual problems.

3. Well-balanced families—spiritually, emotionally, physically, and financially—will create a productive workforce.

4. Strong families study better and create well-educated societies. Education, knowledge, and wisdom are prerequisites for creating and maintaining *globally competitive* countries.

5. The earth and its near *planetary* systems will be preserved and managed much more responsibly than during the past fifty years and have a greater understanding of the systemic and interdependent nature of our solar system.

6. Cohesive family units perpetuate age-old traditions that may otherwise be lost forever.

7. Functionally stable families are a prerequisite for the concept of the family itself—a source of solace, security, unconditional love, and encouragement.

The First Family: How Much Are We Alike?

According to the Bible, the first human family unit God created comprised of Adam and Eve and Cain and Abel. The first case of rebellious attitude, jealousy, and murder occurred in this first family. When Cain became jealous of Abel's offering, which pleased God more than his own, Cain murdered Abel. Almost four thousand years ago, Abraham's nephew, Lot, was made drunk by his two daughters who made their father produce two sons for them because there were no males left in the family due to the destruction of Sodom and Gomorrah.

In the family of Israel's greatest king, David, Amnon, his eldest son, raped his stepsister Tamar, which led Tamar's brother, Absalom, to murder Amnon in a cold-blooded plot. In the same family, David lusted after Bathsheba and committed adultery with her. The Bible is full of stories of every possible spiritual dysfunction that we can think of today—from lies, cheating, and robberies to rape, murder, incest, polygamy, wild orgies, and prostitution.

Nearly three thousand years ago, King Solomon declared, "There is nothing new under the sun" (Ecclesiastes 1:9). This is a strange thought for us when we think of the present state of family units in our world today. The problems of families today are not that far out as many people think. The frequency and magnitude of the problems may be different today, but their basic, underlying nature is not that different. There's a great deal of experiential wisdom on the subject of families during the past six thousand years. It has been passed down from one generation to another, one faith to another, one geographical location to another, and one person to another. "History repeats itself" is a profoundly scientific observation in human organizational systems, including families, which go through cycles of behaviors. Therefore, we can deduce and apply some common principles that are relevant today. There is no need to be overwhelmed by what we see.

Does it make sense to apply the wisdom God gave us for thousands of years to address our contemporary confusion about families? Sometimes, being confused is good; it's a sign of recognition and acceptance. Out of confusion comes clarity. Out of humility comes the power of thinking and the resolve to tackle the family problems. In that sense, we can be optimistic about encountering and fixing the problems of today's families.

What's Missing in Today's Families?

At the fundamental level, today's families may not be any different from those of a century ago—or even six thousand years ago. However, the magnitude of change and rate of change in expectations have altered significantly. I see five major factors missing in today's families.

Two-Parent Structure

It was quite common, just fifty years ago, for a family unit to have both father and mother taking care of their children—and even their parents. Today, unfortunately, a large percentage of family units in the United States and the Western world are headed by a single parent, usually the mother. It takes both parents to raise children to be productive citizens; the absence of a father or mother usually means that an aunt, uncle, or grandparent is raising the children. While their love is not discounted, it's not an ideal substitute for a parent's care, especially when the children reach those tough teenage years when boys are growing into manhood and girls into womanhood. A lack of proper parental guidance in study habits, spirituality, social norms, peer pressure, and healthy entertainment can lead children to rebellion, indifference, selfishness, and immature decisions. The consequences include pre-marital sex, teenage pregnancy, crimes, adultery, and drug addiction.

Most boys grow up to imitate their dads, and most girls become like their mothers. Clearly, when one parent takes on both the roles, it is almost an impossible task. When children grow up in a single-parent family, there's often a lack of emotional stability. Their self-esteem is affected negatively. They are vulnerable to sexual assaults by stepfathers. It is a suboptimal scenario, to say the least.

Quantity Time—Not Just Quality Time

For many years, we have been hearing from some parents that quality time is more important than quantity time. Notwithstanding many practical challenges, especially for single parents, could this be an excuse for covering their guilt for not spending enough time with their children?

It's a well-known fact that children's fundamental beliefs and core values are set firmly before they begin their teenage years. Yet as one or both parents work hard during these early years, their children are deprived of bonding time, which is crucial for building up their core-value base, confidence, etiquette, self-esteem, and citizenship. Of course, many hundreds of parents do not want to be in this situation. They are working very hard—often to just make ends meet. It's become a matter of economic necessity. I also meet parents who have had their children raised in their early years by servants or nannies. In 1993, I was on a flight from Houston to Miami, and the woman sitting next to me was a twenty-four-hour nanny for two young children. She lamented that their parents gave them the comfort of a multimillion-dollar home and all the luxuries you can imagine, but they were essentially being influenced by their peers in school and getting exposed to dangerous habits. She said, "These parents are high-achieving world travelers—very successful professionally, but totally unaware of the negative future they are creating for their young ones."

Active Involvement in Children's Interests

From the twenty-year-olds, I often hear a deep cry that somebody, especially parents, should be more caring about their children's aspirations, activities, and interests: "Our parents don't know or care what's happening in our lives, and they don't seem to want to get involved. They're too busy working too many hours, yet they are shocked when their children are caught in undesirable situations."

The early twenties is one of the most important stages of the life of a young adult. Many famous people, for example, the former chairman of SONY corporation—Akio Morita (1921–1999), Toyota's honorary chairman—Shoichiro Toyoda (1925–2023), the world-famous Elon Musk (1971–), and the influential Methodist preachers of England, John Wesley and Charles Wesley—were all between twenty and twenty-five when they decided to do something significant with their lives.

Isn't it a shame when parents don't know what their youth's goals and interests in life are so that they could encourage them, steer them correctly, and give them moral support? Even though my dad didn't communicate much with me when I was sixteen, I knew I wanted to go into engineering as a career, and he encouraged me to do so. When I graduated and began to work for a company, he knew when and where I was traveling on business. On one of my first trips to the headquarters of the company, I had to stay beyond my itinerary. Even though he was a busy professor, when he came to get me at the airport, and the general manager of the company told my dad that the chairman asked me to stay on for a couple more days on a special assignment, my father was proud. My father went to heaven just before Christmas in 1970 when I was twenty-four years old. I often think of his quiet, but effective, interest and involvement in my teenage years as well as my young adulthood. He and my mom knew all about my sister, Vivian, and me, during all the years they were alive. What a wonderful reflection of gratitude to our parents for their active involvement in our lives. They kept their distance when needed to help us grow, but they stayed close enough to comfort us, strengthen us, and encourage us when we needed that.

Commitment to the Institution of Marriage and Family

Even in America, where nearly 50 percent of marriages end up in a divorce, it's heartening to find some couples who have taken their wedding vows seriously and had blessed marriages for up to sixty years. When we ask these couples for the secret to such durable marriages, they're quick to point out that commitment to the institution of marriage, rooted in sacrificial love, has been on their top three lists.

A wedding is for a day, but marriage is for life. Most couples start out with the notion that marriage will be as romantic and exciting as courtship. Obviously, they have never been instructed or shown that marriage is a continuous improvement journey and not a duplication of the courtship period.

I thought, forty-nine years ago, that marriage would simply be romantic, running around in parks and singing movie songs.

Like most newlyweds, I used to take Chaya out just about daily. During our first year of marriage, we went to parks, movies, and other fun places. After a few months of the fun life, Chaya had a high-risk pregnancy that brought adversity to our few-months-old marriage. On December 18, 1975, at 7:30 p.m., the doctors and nurses monitoring her scared me stiff when they asked me to sign consent papers in case something went seriously wrong. It might have been routine for them to do so, but for me, a student ten thousand miles away from family support, it was a serious thing. Suddenly, I was getting used to the seriousness of responsibilities and deep emotional anxieties, contrary to the bed of roses I had imagined for myself. What I was concerned about most was the safety of Chaya and the baby and my commitment to them both. My prayers to God were the most pleading, mercy-seeking intercessions. We are grateful to God that He answered our anxious prayers and blessed us with our first child, John, at 3:48 a.m. on December 19, 1975. What a blessed Christmas gift in advance.

Today, many people think it's all right to have multiple spouses. The worst-case scenario is when they start out their marriages with the same mindset as leasing, buying, using, and replacing a car. Unfortunately, the divorce laws in the United States have become such that annulling a marriage takes less time in some states than turning in a leased car. Couples can do a no-fault divorce with no questions asked. This phrase, "no-fault divorce," was borrowed from the "no-fault insurance" of the auto insurance industry. What a travesty to the meaning of commitment to marriage.

When a marriage is on the rocks, how can we expect stable emotional relationships at home, in the workplace, or in worship places. People everywhere are walking around with so much despair, despondency, anger, and resentment. They are ready to explode at any time. Was it a surprise to see the 1999 Columbine shootings or the 2004 murder of a ten-year-old student by another student in a Miami school? On February 14, 2018, at Marjory Stoneman Douglas High School in Parkland, Florida, nineteen-year-old Nikolas Cruz, a former student, opened fire, killing seventeen and injuring seventeen more. On March 27, 2023, a former student, twenty-nine-year-old Aiden Hale (formerly Audrey Elizabeth Hale) went into the Covenant School in Nashville and killed six people. Three of the children were nine years old.

America is becoming so violent for children. Are parents losing control of their children? Children from broken homes are the weak links in a nation's productive capacity to create goods and services of the highest quality. The need for a stable family has never been greater. We have moved into an era of a "flat world," as Thomas Friedman calls it, where competition is on a flat playing field. Stable families should be considered an important strategic variable to build the core competencies of a country for economic competitiveness.

Formal Education about Raising Families

There were no formal courses on raising families in high schools, colleges, or universities when I was a youth. Most of us have learned the "art of marriage" by trial and error. Even in the major research and teaching university I've been a faculty member at for more than four decades, there are no formal courses to prepare students for the marriage journey. Mostly, it's only those who get married in a church or other religious institutions who are required to attend six to eight sessions before the wedding ceremony is solemnized. Preventing the breakup of marriages is so much easier and less costly to society than waiting for emotional, financial, and physical disasters to strike.

Community colleges and universities can easily offer a "marriage readiness certificate" in the departments of education, psychology, or religion. This could help reduce the divorce rate in the next generation.

What's Needed to Build and/or Rebuild Our Families?

Reworking a product that's not up to specifications is a difficult and costly process, but it's better to fix it late than never. You never know who's going to be using that product. A family is much more significant than a product, but the analogy is relevant.

Genichi Taguchi, a famous Japanese quality expert, came up with the concept of "quality loss function" in the 1980s. It says that every defective product creates a loss to society in some way or another. He came up with statistical approaches to minimize losses. Ford Motor Company was one of the earliest adopters of his philosophy. If we extrapolate his concept to families, we can glean some interesting insights. What if every family must strive to minimize the total social cost (or loss) of the world by designing, developing, and managing its spiritual, emotional, physical, and financial aspects in an optimal manner? When we buy a product or service, we expect to get the most value for our money. When we buy or build a house, should we not expect the best value (spiritually, emotionally, physically, and financially) from the family units in the neighborhood since those family units affect ours?

When we build a new family, it's a bit easier than rebuilding that is dysfunctional because of its defective design, development, or maintenance. No one starts out by saying, "We can tolerate a drug-addicted child." No company says, "We can make a defective automobile." Can we actually design, develop, and maintain a family that minimizes the social cost to our world? The answer is yes—even when wholesome, traditional, two-parent families are so rare. There are some fundamental requirements for creating and sustaining "high-performance families" (HPFs). These are briefly clarified below, and the many facets of these factors are detailed in the rest of this book:

1. Follow the Family Design Manual daily.
2. Build or rebuild families for *significance* and not just for success.
3. Constantly recognize the societal impact.

4. Shape your family as a system and not as a component.
5. Take responsibility for your family collectively and as a community.
6. Celebrate your family's achievements consistently.
7. Learn and apply diligently the art and science of family management.

1. Follow the Family Design Manual daily. God, as the Creator of the first family unit of Adam and Eve gave us the first "Family Design Manual" (the Holy Bible), which He authored over a 1,600-year period with about forty individuals, including Moses, Isaiah, Jeremiah, Daniel, Ezekiel, Samuel, Ezra, Nehemiah, King David, King Solomon, Matthew, John, Paul, Peter, James, and Jude.

Just as we refer to a product manual when we need to fix it or obtain its optimal performance, we need to refer to the Bible and read all its relevant sections to create and sustain HPFs. It's that simple. Then why don't we do it? We don't do it for many reasons:

1. Many people don't know the Bible offers this help. They think it's a religious book.
2. Those who read the Bible don't read all of it. They only read a few passages or verses they're familiar with, comfortable with, or want to believe selectively.
3. Some churches do not believe in the inerrancy and infallibility of the entire Bible and do not teach their members all the truths of the Bible. And, as the familiar adage goes, "half knowledge is dangerous."
4. Many individuals do not read or study the Bible with the same interest, diligence, and passion as they read other books and novels. It's a lack of true belief that the entire Bible was authored by the inspiration of God through the Holy Spirit (2 Timothy 3:16). The Word of God is living and powerful, and it is sharper than a two-edged sword (Hebrews 4:12).

2. Build or rebuild families for significance and not success. Most parents teach their children to become successful at whatever they want to be—engineers, doctors, teachers, nurses, lawyers, technicians, politicians, police officers, or firefighters—but success is fleeting, temporary, and not ultimately fulfilling. This is one of major causes of families breaking apart at the seams at the pinnacle of their careers.

Success lasts only for a while, and dissatisfaction sets in quickly, especially with fame and fortune. Countless famous people have seen breakups of their marriages, family units, and careers. Once the fame or fortune wears off, people resort to mood-altering substances, which destroy their bodies, minds, and relationships.

Mother Teresa epitomized seeking significance and not success. She demonstrated unselfish love toward the downtrodden for all her life. She had the fame, was a Nobel-Prize winner, and was extremely simple and austere. She used to have two saris: one to wear and the other to be washed. Since she sought significance, success followed in her worldwide ministry. The impact of her life is unquestioned. Today, the legacy of her philosophy of loving and taking care of the downtrodden continues in more than eighty-five countries. That's significance. The most fulfilled people are those who pursue significance and not success. Parents who create families for significance are wise and unselfish. Their outlook has produced some of the most significant people in history.

3. Constantly recognize the societal impact. Families are the fundamental units of societies. Therefore, we have an obligation, as responsible and responsive citizens, to create and sustain our families as a part of a much larger role: to offer productive individuals from our families to our societies. We're giving back something in return for providing us an economic, emotional, physical, and spiritual support system.

Families create human links to the chain of humanity. The chain is only as strong its weakest link. How many of these weakest links have been created by your family? Are you contributing to the strength of humanity by bringing up children you can be very proud of? Once we start thinking like this, we'll be more conscious of our roles as fathers, mothers, sons, daughters, and grandchildren.

Events shape the history of our world. Major events shape new and relevant norms through paradigm shifts. For example, 9/11 was such a major event that continues to change the way we do many things in life, including street cameras, card scans, iris and finger-touch entry to buildings. It changed air travel and shipping of goods and services. A few individuals negatively changed society and reshaped the immigration policies to a point where some prominent universities had to operate their physics and chemistry labs at 60 percent capacity. The loss of scientists and engineers in the United States due to 9/11 has been enormous, and the social cost is immeasurable.

4. Shape your family as a system and not as a component. By definition, a system is a set of interrelated components or parts. When one component is affected, the entire system is affected as well. For example, the hydraulic cylinder that lowers the wheels before landing an airplane is part of the landing gear system. If the reliability of this hydraulic component is poor, and it fails to do its function, the entire landing gear system is inoperable. Even though the pilot can do an emergency landing on the belly of the plane, very few people would want to be on that plane. Think of each family as an extremely important component of the system of families in the world. If we have two billion family units in world nearing eight billion people that's lots of families. When we manage our particular family unit, we try to make their lives as comfortable as possible. Families need to function with high reliability so that our global family functions optimally, taking care of the oceans, lakes, forests, animals, birds, and everything else placed under our care on this planet by our heavenly Father. When we bring up our children as honest, responsible individuals, their decisions and actions have positive effects on this earth we all share. Can you imagine how many millions have perished just during the past fifty years because of the wrong values, attitudes, and decisions of a few family units? Selfish, greedy, and egotistical leaders have been responsible for millions of human deaths.

5. *Take responsibility for your family collectively and as a community.* Our hearts went out to a father when my wife and I met him years ago. He deeply touched more than four hundred students and faculty members by narrating the tragic Columbine massacre of 1999. Two twelfth-grade students shot to death ten young students and a teacher, and his daughter was one of the victims. Could the parents of the young perpetrators of this massacre have been more responsible to their community by raising their boys with positive self-esteem and tolerant attitude toward other student's religious beliefs? Families must be required to raise their children with a sense of community. When one family member is affected, everyone in the community is too. We see this community mindset in certain parts of the country more than the others—for various reasons. It is the responsibility of all families in the community to make sure everyone else's interests are respected. When families become selfish and greedy, their communities suffer.

6. *Celebrate your family's achievements.* To give our families HPF status, it's necessary to celebrate all important events in our families—past, present, and future. Celebrations don't have to be expensive. They must be timely. Even a short telephone call to a college child on their birthday could be a celebration because it's a recognition of the importance of that day when they were given as a gift to the family from God—to be loved, cherished, and encouraged. Many parents give expensive "guilt gifts," including cars, but many parents don't even take the time to say, "I love you" to their children. Affirmative words are only seconds long, yet they seem to be rare. This goes for children celebrating their parents' birthdays, Mother's Day, Father's Day, and anniversaries.

Most positive reinforcement occasions are short and sweet, but they have a positive and profound impact on the lives of those in the family who have been recognized and affirmed. Every affirmation is like a coat of paint that adds to the protection of the individual's sense of serenity, which is a prerequisite for stable families. If a family celebrates its pet's birthday, but ignores its child's birthday, that's a suboptimal family.

7. Learn and apply the art and science of family management. Family management is mostly an art and partly a science. To build or rebuild HPFs, family management must be taught formally at the high school, college, and university levels. When that's done, we may see the emergence of family management as an evolving science. The principles can be discovered, rediscovered, and taught so that we will have stronger and more stable families, communities, and countries. I hope that others join forces with like-minded people to create single courses, multiple-course certificate programs, and the like to create more books, journals, and scientific reports.

This book proposes many-time tested principles for creating, nurturing, and sustaining HPFs according to thousands of years of biblical wisdom. God gives us a further understanding and knowledge to develop additional truths and principles based on His prescriptions. The search for *Family by the Bible* is a continuous mindset and not a static, one-shot deal.

The art and science of family management, as suggested here, is based on the power of the living, omnipotent (all-powerful), omniscient (present everywhere), sovereign (in control of all events), loving, and just God. The foundation of this family management concept must be established in the following ways:

1. regular and consistent prayers to the one living God (YHWH)
2. obedience to Jesus's two commandments: "Love the Lord your God with all your heart, soul, and mind" and "Love your neighbor as yourself"
3. guidance by the Holy Spirit, the Comforter, and the Third Person of the Godhead

Three Actions I Can Take for One Month after Reading This Chapter

    1.
    2.
    3.

Chapter Two
FAMILY MANAGEMENT

Let deacons be the husbands of one wife, ruling
their children and their own houses well.
—1 TIMOTHY 3:12

In chapter 1, we set the stage for the need to rebuild our families if they're broken, and to build them right the first time if we're starting out to do so. Beginning with this chapter, I'll present the more specifics of what I call "family management," (FM), which is a deliberate, systematic, continuous, process of creating, and sustaining a family unit for significance.

The key words in this definition are highlighted to emphasize their importance. Thus, by its very definition, I consider family management (FM) as a deliberate (not accidental or matter of fact); a systematic (not random or haphazard), and a continuously sustaining process. What's the main purpose of FM?—to create a family unit, and to sustain it for Significance (not merely for success). We define a family unit here as husband and wife, and their children. When a husband or wife is deceased, two general scenarios would ensue: widowhood for life or, re-marriage. When a re-marriage occurs and children are born from it, the new family structure is still a family unit.

The Seven Similarities of Families and Enterprises

For some, the word *management* may not associate well with *family*. It seems like we are talking about companies or enterprises and their management. Interestingly, every family unit can be viewed as an enterprise, and the advantage of doing so is that we can apply most, if not all, the concepts of enterprise management in our families.

First, let us look at the common characteristics of enterprises and families. Then I'll clarify the advantages of treating families as enterprises when it comes to making them high-performance families (HPFs). These are the most important similarities of families and enterprises (companies, schools, colleges, universities, hospitals, government organizations):

1. People: Both enterprises and families are comprised of people. Every enterprise, such as a one-person consulting sole proprietorship or an S-corporation, is no different from a family unit of one or more members. Since people are people, the fundamental nature of problems of the family are the same: creating an environment for effective and efficient utilization of resources available, including people, money, materials, energy, and technologies. Just as a company experiences internal politics, a family unit, especially one with many members, can see destructive forces tear apart the group. What about jealousies, resentments, and competitiveness? Have you seen them in families and enterprises?

Because human nature is the same in family units and enterprises, the nature of managerial issues is often similar—if not the same. The magnitude of the problems may vary, but their causes may not be that different.

More similarities exist between the peoples of the world than differences. This assertion is based on my personal observations during the past fifty-six years in more than one hundred countries, representing almost 75 percent the gross national product of the world. Therefore, the fundamental models of management are not vastly different between countries, companies, or families.

2. Limited Resources: An enterprise does not have unlimited resources such as money, capital, materials, manpower, energy, technology, information, and knowledge, and a family unit is limited in all of these. Because the concept of management evolved over millennia to manage limited resources to accomplish goals and objectives in enterprises, it seems perfectly appropriate to talk about the applications of management theory and practice to family units.

Virtually every major concept presented in the management literature may be applied to families. For example, consider customer focus. The stakeholders of a family unit are its *internal customers* (family members and employees) and *external customers* (teachers, classmates, friends, relatives, preachers, and employers). Just as in corporations, there is a need to satisfy all these stakeholders with limited available resources.

With budgetary planning, time management, inventory control, facilities planning, and layout principles in maintaining smooth traffic flow and energy efficiency in home construction, hospitality management of guests for parties and vacations, the management of limited resources like money, time, and physical and emotional energy is critical. Families want to minimize stress. Many families suffer from sleep deprivation, disharmony, and lack of focus as a result of improper management of their limited resources.

3. Communication: Whether it's Wal-Mart or a three-member family unit, communication is the most important attribute. My fifty-four years of teaching, consulting, preaching, counseling, and training shows that almost 90 percent of problems in enterprises and families are about communication: lack of communication, overcommunication, under-communication, untimely communication, improper communication, and hasty communication. In every managerial function—planning, organizing, leading, motivating, delegating, and controlling—communication is needed. Without it, none of these managerial functions can be executed. There's so much research available about communication in psychology, sociology, anthropology, systems theory, and cybernetics literature.

Every problem in families can be traced directly or indirectly to communication. While so many practical and proven ideas have been proposed by God Almighty, through His Word, we ignore them because we think the Bible is just a religious book. In my humble opinion, God's wisdom transcends all scientific disciplines. He's the "master designer," and He created the brains of His creation. They, in turn, create the concepts of every discipline.

4. Environment: Every government, company, or enterprise has to operate in an environment that is political, economic, social, cultural, and ecological in nature. A family unit is no different. It also operates within these confines and constraints.

Families and their members have to abide by all the major laws at the local, state, and federal levels—just as corporations have to. There are penalties and costs associated with the violation of these laws. God formulated many principles that can help families respect their political, economic, cultural, social, and ecological environments. We have not been exposed to them or taught in a systematic manner. The subsequent chapters of this book allude to God's wisdom on the responsibilities toward and involvement in our environment.

5. Moral Excellence: Common to enterprises and families is morality. Ethics-related, conscience-bound human traits enable corporations and family units to perpetuate commonly held values of human dignity, fairness, justice, and responsible freedom. *Corporate governance* has moved from a buzzword to business lingo just during the past ten or fifteen years because of corporate ethics scandals, including Enron and Anderson. Many family scandals occur every day; they're often protected by the privacy of families, but every now and then, they become big news—be it the rich, royal, and famous or the poor and ordinary.

One of the famous stories of moral indiscretion with serious consequences for generations happened three thousand years ago. King David committed adultery by taking the wife of his soldier, Uriah, and then plotting his death in the battlefield in a repulsive manner. Just as some individuals at Enron had to go to jail, the cost of David's deviation from God's standard of moral excellence was staggering. His son, Amnon, followed his dad's example and raped his stepsister, Tamar. In revenge, Tamar's brother, Absalom, one of David's favorite sons, murdered Amnon. The sword never departed from David's house, and he wasn't allowed by God to build the Holy Temple he planned. Further, the kingdom of Israel was divided up after Solomon's idolatry to multiple pagan gods. There is no free lunch, and God's blessings on families require obedience to His moral excellence. He is holy and just, and He is a loving God.

6. Change: Every organization and family changes. The only thing constant is change—from the time of conception until death. From the time a company is founded, it evolves physically, economically, and culturally. Every enterprise goes through a life cycle curve, or "S-curve," in four stages: A (initiation), B (growth), C (saturation), and D (decay) (figure 2.1).

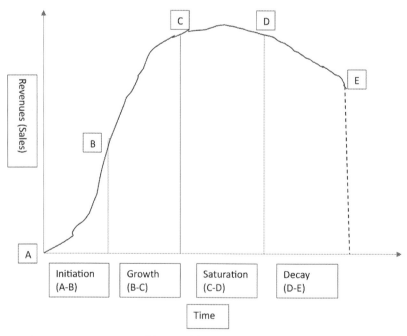

Fig. 2.1 The S-Curve

After the initial startup (stage A), a company grows quickly (stage B). At some point, it reaches an almost flat saturation (stage C), and then it begins to decay (stage D).

During the 1970s, I used to fly Braniff, Ozark, National, TWA, and Pan Am. The first three airlines decayed within a few years; Pan Am, survived about sixty-four years (1927–1991). We don't hear about Studebaker (a 1950s auto company) or Eastern Airlines, which went bankrupt in the 1980s. All organizations and countries have their glory days (stage B), but at some point, they saturate, decay, and die. The same is true with families and the individuals therein. We are born, grow rapidly, mature, get old, and die. This is the general pattern of the human life cycle. Of course, there are exceptions, like premature births and deaths, but families must prepare to manage change. Change is inevitable. It's not an *if* thing. It's a *how* thing.

The beautiful part of change is that God has a very clean approach to managing the change process in a believer's life. Therefore, families can view change management in a positive way rather than a negative one. God has a plan to manage this life and the life after it—for those who accept His plan. Chapter 12 deals with the various stages of life and the many major changes in those stages.

7. Problems: I define a problem as "a significant, perceived, negative deviation of experience from expectation." Not all perceived negative deviations between experiences and expectations are problems—only those that are perceived to be significant. For example, you get ready to go to work, get in your car, and turn on the ignition. The car doesn't start. If you have no critical, in-person appointments until after lunch, and you estimate that it will take about forty-five minutes for the roadside assistance to help jump-start or replace the battery, you won't consider this a problem—even though there is a negatively perceived difference between your usual expectation and your experience. On the other hand, if you had a very important presentation, and no one else was qualified to give it, the perceived negative deviation is significant. Therefore, you'll perceive this situation as a problem. Thus, all issues are not problems, but all

problems are issues. Just as every enterprise has problems every day, every family has its own problems too:

1. internal politics, jockeying for position or power, gossip, jealousies, pettiness, backsliding
2. competing for limited resources (people, machines/equipment, materials, and money)
3. expecting rewards without expecting performance
4. cynicism (of new initiatives)
5. disloyalty
6. ingratitude
7. complacency
8. undermining authority
9. poor motivation
10. poor performance
11. low morale

To conclude this chapter, we see that there are many similarities between enterprises and families. Therefore, family management, as an essential approach to manage families, is logical and reasonable. The many theories and practical principles that have worked effectively in enterprises can be applied to family units as well.

The Seven Managerial Functions in a Family Unit

There are seven commonly recognized managerial functions in an enterprise or a family unit (figure 2.2):

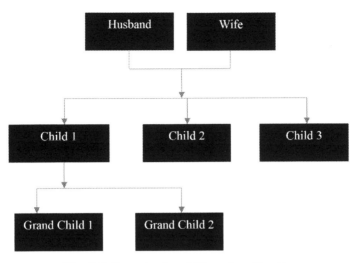

Fig. 2.2 Organizational Chart for a Family

1. planning
2. organizing
3. leading
4. motivating
5. delegating
6. controlling
7. communicating

The seventh function—communicating—is common to the other six. We cannot do any of them without communication.

Chapters 3–10 talk about these functions in detail. They are crucial for managing the family unit and realizing the potential God has placed in them. The first managerial function in a family unit is communication.

Three Actions I Can Take for One Month after Reading This Chapter

1.
2.
3.

Chapter Three
COMMUNICATION

A word fitly spoken is like apples of gold in settings of silver.
—PROVERBS 5:11

The first thing God did after creating Adam was *communicate* with him:

> And the Lord God commanded the man saying, "Of every tree of the garden, you may freely eat; but of the tree of the knowledge of good and evil you shall not eat, for in the day that you eat of it you shall surely die." (Genesis 2:16–17)

This communication from God was very clear:

> Adam could enjoy any fruit of the trees, except the one excluded. The consequence of disobeying God was going to be death if the fruit of the tree of knowledge was eaten.

God gave the gift of freedom to choose alternatives and the blessings and consequences for each of them. Eve was deceived by Satan (in serpent form), and she ate the forbidden fruit and shared it with Adam. They both realized they had disobeyed God. His communication was clear. The result was the shame of sin. Even in this first disobedience, God was merciful not to make them die. He clothed them in tunics, pronounced physical death for Adam and Eve, and cursed the serpent. When God confronted Adam about the forbidden fruit, he blamed Eve. When God asked Eve, she blamed the serpent (Genesis 3). Deliberate noncompliance to a communicated instruction leads to excuses. This happens in every family and in every enterprise. As pointed out before, most problems center around communication.

The Most Important Function

Communication is the common function for the other six managerial functions of a family, and it's also the most important one. Without communication, nothing happens. Communication executes ideas into action, expresses emotions, builds or breaks relationships, and confronts or comforts. They argue or appease. They love or hate. Communication is the key to designing, developing, and maintaining family units.

The Ten Types of Communication

Many problems arise during communication. Here are the most common communication problems:

1. lack of communication
2. miscommunication
3. untimely communication
4. overcommunication
5. under-communication
6. hasty communication
7. inappropriate (irrelevant, insensitive) communication

8. silent communication
9. misleading communication
10. defensive communication

Lack of Communication

Our very dear friends Marie and Ray allowed my wife and me to share about a situation that can be an excellent reminder to avoid this type of communication. On Marie's special birthday, Ray wanted to surprise her with a beautiful bouquet of flowers. Without telling her, Ray took the little dog that Marie was dog-sitting with him to the florist. Marie panicked. She was looking for the little dog all over the house, calling out, and going out to the street. With her apprehension turning into anxiety and then into worry, she began to cry and pray. Ray walks in with a big smile on his face, expecting to see Marie's reaction when she receives the flowers. When she saw the little dog, she was furious. "Why didn't you tell me that you took the dog with you?" Ray didn't think it was important to say, "Honey, I am taking the dog with me." It took a while for Marie to appreciate the beautiful flowers Ray had spent a fortune on. Doesn't this happen to all of us at one time or another?

Miscommunication

This common problem occurs because of the noise (distortion) in the message between the person sending the message and the one receiving it (figure 3.1)

Fig. 3.1 Basic Communication Process, with Distortion

Miscommunication is when a distortion in the message occurs by the way the message was sent, transmitted, or received. The way the recipient perceives the message is dictated by state of mind, background knowledge, and transmission difficulties.

Many studies exist on nonverbal communication and body language. The powerful "7-38-55 rule" was developed by Dr. Albert Mehrabian, a professor emeritus of psychology at the University of California, Los Angeles. The renowned behavioral psychologist says that 7 percent of all communication is verbal, 38 percent is nonverbal, and 55 percent is body language, including facial expressions. These three forms must be congruent. When we write a letter or an email or talk on the telephone, there is a high possibility for miscommunication. You can easily recall the times when you meant your message to be one way, but you were totally misunderstood—even in face-to-face conversation. You can imagine how much worse the misunderstanding is when the communication occurs nonverbally.

One effective way to minimize miscommunication and misunderstanding is to state the intent of your message up front so that the recipient of the message can interpret your message in the context of that intent. When we don't do so, it's often too late to clarify our intent—and the damage has been done.

In the Bible, there was a major miscommunication between Abraham's son, Isaac, and Isaac's second son, Jacob, who deceived his father through the initiative of his mother, Rebekah. She deceptively put Esau's clothes on Jacob, including the skins of kid goats on his hands and the smooth part of his neck. She concealed Jacob's body language because Isaac didn't have good eyesight in his old age. Jacob lied four times to his father, saying he was Esau when he was not.

Untimely Communication

In December 1970, my uncle was disappointed, sad, and angry that the news about his only brother's demise wasn't communicated to him for nearly a week after it happened. One of his close relatives asked someone to send a telegram to him. In the 1970s, that was a common way to communicate in India, but my uncle did not receive the telegram for more than a week. If he had gotten it within twenty-four hours or even forty-eight hours, he said, "I'd have flown from New York to be there in Hyderabad (India) for the funeral services." This was the case where the communication was untimely because it was too late.

Equally bad can be untimely communication when it is too soon. When my father passed away suddenly from a heart attack, my grandfather, who was almost eighty years old, wasn't woken up to be informed because of the fear of causing him a sudden shock when his own health was not very good. If the message about my dad's death had been conveyed sooner than necessary, there could've been a problem. So, he was informed slowly the next day. My grandfather was more than shocked, but at least he didn't have a heart attack himself.

Overcommunication

Overcommunication is a serious problem. Joseph, the eleventh son of Jacob, was an example of overcommunicating. He received a special colored coat from his dad, and his brothers hated him. He was talking about his dream to his brothers, and they began to develop envy toward him (Genesis 37:3–11). Overcommunication occurs when we feel superior, have a gossiping tongue, or embellish what we heard from someone else.

Under-Communication

Withholding the vital part of a message is under-communication, and this can lead to problems in families and relationships. Under-communication occurs because of fear of negative consequences, a reprisal, or a financial loss. A common example of this is when a husband doesn't tell his wife that he was introduced to a unmarried female colleague at work. If the husband doesn't say anything about this casual incident to his wife, it could lead to problems. In a social engagement a couple of weeks later, the colleague might say, "I met your husband. He's so kind and gentle. I like him." Well, that's going to be a long night for the husband, at the very least, or having to sleep on a couch, at the very worst.

Hasty Communication

This common form of communication is a reason for so many challenges in families. I am the first to admit that I am guilty of this type of communication with my wife. Isn't it interesting that we communicate hastily at home more readily than in workplace or social settings? It's because we take our family members for granted. We don't think that their reactions are that important. We think they'll understand every time. In the early stages of a family unit, perhaps it is. As time goes on, hasty communication results in walls of indifference. A simple, practical way to minimize the hasty communication is "TBYA" (think before you act). Before saying something, ask, "What are the possible consequences of saying this?"

In the Bible, Peter was an impetuous, hasty communicator. After the Lord's Supper, on the night He was betrayed by Judas Iscariot, the Lord tells Peter that He prayed for him that his faith should not fail, and that when he returned to Him, to strengthen his brethren. Peter said, "Lord, I am ready to go with You, both to prison and to death." Jesus said, "I tell you, Peter, the rooster shall not crow this day before you will deny three times that you know Me" (Luke 22:32–34).

Inappropriate (Irrelevant, Insensitive) Communication

Being relevant in communication is a positive trait. Any irrelevant communication is inappropriate. Social norms have changed so much during the past ten years that what was considered inappropriate communication then is now accepted as OK. Ten years ago, students didn't have to be told not to use profane language in class discussions. Today, they must be warned ahead of time. The extent to which verbal pollution is tolerated in our societies is astonishing. I hope there will be laws against verbal pollution just as we have for smoking. After all, shouldn't our children be brought up in a verbally decent language environment?

Silent Communication

We may not usually think of this as a form of communication, yet it's one of the toughest ones to understand. Other than body language, no other form of expression can be understood here. Sulking, pouting, and rolling eyes are common modes of silent communication. No words said can mean a lot is not said. Silent communication usually follows an argument, intense discussion, or festering resentment. A short period of such communication may be a good thing—to calm down and not escalate the conflict. Holding unexpressed resentment is not good for anyone's health. A proper time and place must be found to vent unexpressed anger and feelings. Silent communication can be used to get things done without discussion, to manipulate, or to punish. This type of communication can tear apart relationships if it is not addressed in a timely manner.

Misleading Communication

This is a very damaging form of communication. Even though the armed forces regularly use misleading communication and disinformation against their enemies or adversaries, it can create serious problems for families.

Misleading communication occurs when the sender of the message deliberately distorts the message so that the recipient is misled in thinking or action. We are not talking about practical jokes on April

Fool's Day or surprise parties. Misleading communication often results in family disputes and causes rifts for generations. A common setting for misleading communication is in wills, inheritance, and estate matters. So many families split apart after serious incidents of misleading communication.

Defensive Communication

This common form of communication sets up barricades to the true intent and content of the message. People say, "I don't think it'll work," "We've tried that before—it won't work," or "You told me that a thousand times before." These are a few examples of defensive communication. It is a natural response to the fear of change, especially apprehension about security. It's the first reaction to resistance to change. One practical way to minimize this is to explain the benefits to all who could be affected by a particular suggestion.

The Two Fundamental Mechanisms in Any Type of Communication

We have seen the ten types of communication, and there are two basic mechanisms: open-loop mechanism and closed-loop mechanism.

Open-Loop Mechanism

In the context of communication, the open-loop concept is from the control theory. It's taken from the systems control theory. There is so much information available about electrical engineering and cybernetics. For a simple explanation of open loop communication, see figure 3.2.

Fig. 3.2 Open-Loop Mechanism

The message is received with or without distortion during the transmission process, but there is no feedback from the receiver to the sender. A common example of this mechanism in action is at drive-through banks or fast-food restaurants. After I deposited a check, the teller completed the transaction, but didn't say, "Have a good day." There was no indication that the transaction was indeed completed. At a drive-through restaurant, the order was handed to me without saying anything. I wasn't sure if the order was completed or not. To make sure, I said, "Thank you."

If a parent tells a child to do something important by a certain time, but the child says, "I am tied up with something urgent, but I'll have that done for you as soon as I am done," the parent will be appreciative. If the parent sees that the task is not done—with no response from the child—there will be unnecessary scolding and further aggravation because it was open-loop communication with no feedback on the part of the child.

Closed-Loop Communication

This type of communication incorporates *feedback* as shown in figure 3.3.

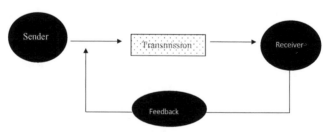

Fig. 3.3 Closed-Loop Mechanism of Communication

Closed-loop communication overcomes the problem of a lack of feedback. In the previously discussed example, when the child gives a feed back to the parent's instruction, the parent will feel respected.

Samuel went to his mentor, Eli, thinking that *he* called him in the night, and Eli perceived that God was calling Samuel because he wasn't. Eli instructed Samuel (with a little feedback) to say, "Here I am Lord" the next time he was called. When God called Samuel again, that's what he did. Eli was curious about the feedback from Samuel and asked him what God said. Unfortunately, what Samuel shares with Eli wasn't pleasant news because God was warning that trouble awaits Eli's family because of the sins of his sons Hophni and Phinehas (1 Samuel 3). By sharing the feedback about God's communication with him, Samuel was spared any ill will on the part of Eli.

As a rule of thumb, try your best to incorporate the closed-loop mechanism in your communications.

Private versus Public Reprimand

At one time or another, every child, and adult needs correction in a family unit. Correction must be done caringly, promptly, and privately.

Caringly

It's important that correction is never done with a punishing or vindictive attitude. The objective of correction is to make a person change their behavior for the better and not for the worse. When children are corrected with a punishing attitude, they become indifferent and then rebellious. In the worst case, they shut others off for years. When correcting caringly, you need the right intent and motive.

Promptly

If corrective action is postponed, the person being corrected perceives weakness, lack of authority, and/or moral courage. King David did not correct his son Amnon promptly after the latter raped his half sister, Tamar. This set into motion a number of events in David's family, starting with the murder of Amnon by David's other son, Absalom. The sword never departed from David's family.

Privately

Many parents spank their children in public. Many grown-ups scold their employees in public, causing irreparable emotional damage. It is extremely important that children and adults are corrected in private. My formula for an effective private reprimand is *PCP* (figure 3.4):

1. praise
2. critique
3. praise

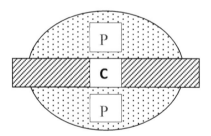

Fig. 3.4 Sumanth's "Sandwich Formula" for Private Reprimand

Praise

First, praise—genuinely and briefly—for whatever the person has been doing well before the need for correction arose.

Critique

Next, ask, "Why did you do what you did?" Upon receiving the answer, ask them, "What do you plan to do to prevent this from happening again?" If the mistake requires compensation, ask, "How do you plan to compensate for the lost performance?" Note that the critique has been done through a questioning process and not a statement. This gives feedback for their behavior. Saying "I can't believe you've done this," "How can you be so unintelligent?" or "I don't want to see you repeat this again!" makes the person feel miserable and resentful. Keep the critique time very low compared to the praise time before and after. It's like the one-patty sandwich wherein the bread above and below the patty is much thicker. Spending less time on the critique part than the praise part makes the person feel responsible and remorseful about their behavior.

Praise

Finally, praise the person again by reaffirming their good behavior or good performance prior to this incident. When that person leaves, they should feel that this one negative episode is not going to discolor all the good things done in the past.

I have been applying my sandwich formula successfully since 1969 when I first used it to privately reprimand a third-shift worker in a big corporation. I also applied it in my family when correcting my children. It works.

Conflicts between Spouses

No marriage is perfect. No family communicates perfectly. If someone says otherwise, they're not being honest with you or themselves. Since the administrative leaders of a family unit should be husband and wife, communication problems between them can result in conflicts. While conflicts cannot be completely avoided, they can be minimized—and their negative impact can be eliminated if resolved properly.

A conflict arises from a difference of opinion. This difference of opinion may be spiritual, emotional, physical, and/or financial. A 2021 study reported that 40 percent of American family households have significant financial problems (Chris Massman, a licensed marriage and family therapist, "7 Common Types of Family Problems and How to Deal with Them," Feb. 1, 2022). The number one issue for families is *money*. If the husband is the sole breadwinner and the wife is the home engineer—who designs, develops, and maintains the home—conflicts about money matters can be frequent and nasty. It's easy for a husband to think that his wife is wasting her time and his money because she is home. A wife might resent the fact that her husband gets professional recognition while she works hard around the house. She might feel like she is not respected.

What does the Bible suggest for conflicts between husband and wife? The Bible asks the husband to love his wife and the wife to submit to her husband (Ephesians 5:25). The word "submission" is ultimately derived from the Latin "*submittere*," which means "to lower, reduce, yield." We submit first to God, then to His Word, and then to our families, neighbors, community, and society. The word "submit" here is grossly misunderstood by women—and even by staunch Christians.

The concept of yielding in the submission has a significance when you think about it. On the highway, you yield when coming in from a side ramp. You haven't given up your freedom or right to drive; you've simply acknowledged the right of way for the speeding car on the highway. That's the same in marriage. The wife is not asked to submit to husband out of fear. She is to respect her husband's role as assigned by God in the Garden of Eden—as a coequal but different in the roles God assigned them. Husbands value respect and love from their wives, and wives desire caring, sensitive love and respect from their husbands.

Thus, to prevent a conflict from happening or to resolve it, it is biblical for both the husband and wife to ask a fundamental question: "Has this conflict come because we violated God's prescription for our different yet significant roles?"

Conflicts between Siblings

The first conflict between Cain and Abel, the first two sons of Adam and Eve, was rooted in jealousy. Cain saw that God respected Abel's offering but not his offering (Genesis 4:4–5). Cain struck down Abel and committed the first murder in recorded human history. The jealousy factor is especially strong in families with many children, stepchildren, and favoritism by one or both parents.

Esau and Jacob, the twin sons of Isaac and Rebecca, seemed destined for conflict in their mother's womb:

> And the Lord said to her: "Two nations are in your womb, two peoples shall be separated from your body, one people shall be stronger than the other, And the older shall serve the younger." (Genesis 25:23)

Rebecca played the favorites with Jacob and made him deceive his father and steal his brother Esau's blessing. As expected, Esau hated Jacob for this. Rebecca instructed Jacob to flee from Esau to her brother Laban in Haran. She thought Esau's anger would come down and then Jacob could return soon. Well, that soon became many years. Eventually, Esau forgave his brother (Genesis 33). Esau showed and placed his priority correctly. A loving relationship between a husband and a wife sets an example for their children.

Most rivalries, pettiness, jealousy, and strained relationships between siblings carry forward into their children's lives—and even into their grandchildren's lives. The sense of family and emotional support mechanism are often lost. Blood is thicker than water, and when life gets tough, we may crave togetherness with our extended families. Siblings come from the same blood. Therefore, it's in their long-term interests that they avoid conflicts, but if they do get into them, they must resolve them amiably and honorably.

Conflicts between Parents and Children

A parent and child who love each other so much during early childhood can have relational challenges during the teen years and adult stages. Deep emotional scars remain in grown-ups because of conflicts with one or both parents when they were children, young adults, and/or married adults.

Some critical factors cause conflicts between parents and children:

1. lack of trust
2. lack of respect
3. lack of tough love

Lack of Trust

Most often, the child-parent relationship suffers setbacks during the early teenage years when boys and girls are growing physically and emotionally into manhood or womanhood. Often, they are confused and try to fit in with their friends. They may seem aloof with their parents, seeking to assert their own identities, and their interests are quite different from their parents' interests.

The ten types of communication become evident at this stage, and conflicts arise. During the difficult transition to young adulthood, teenagers want trust. They want their parents to trust them fully.

The parents say, "How can we trust you when your friends have such different values from what we've so carefully imparted for ten, fifteen, or sixteen years? How can we trust you when you're interested in friends who are so far away in their mannerisms, beliefs, and potential?" Today's warped freedoms make life complex for adults, children, and adolescents.

Respect

Parents yearn for respect more than anything else during those terrible teenage years. They don't want their children to talk back, they want them to look at them while they're saying something to them, and they want to feel that their opinions and advice matter while the teenagers seek advice from friends and peers.

Tough Love

Dr. James Dobson, a well-known American Evangelical Christian author and psychologist founded Focus on the Family Ministries. He says that families need to practice tough love, which is caring but disciplined. Love has boundaries. Tough love seems harsh, but it requires a long-term view of the good and the bad. Tough love means saying no to negative things and negative choices. Dobson says, "Love is not an emotion—it's a choice." That makes so much sense. In Western society, we use the term *love* so loosely that we don't seem to understand the true depth of its meaning. True love, which is often manifested in tough love, means making the conscious decision to care for someone and be willing to give them consequences for their wrong choices—even when they don't want to hear about them. Parents practicing tough love become true friends to their children—no matter their ages.

King Solomon's proverbs outlined the benefits and pitfalls of tough love. God showed His tough love toward King David when he committed adultery with Bathsheba. God confronted David about his sin, and punishment followed.

Dobson advises parents to be patient through the teenage years of their children. By about nineteen, they come back full circle, admiring the wise counsel of their parents, as they used to when they were young. The teenage transition is probably the toughest one in life. Dobson's advice is very well placed and appreciated. His bestsellers *Raising Boys* and *Raising Girls* are valuable for parents.

What does the Bible suggest for resolving conflicts between parents and children? Paul advises: "Children: obey your parents in the Lord, for this is right."

"Honor your father and mother" is the first commandment with a promise that it may be well with you and may live long on the earth (Ephesians 6:1–3). Paul says, "Do not provoke your children to wrath, but bring them up in the training and admonition of the Lord" (Ephesians 6:4).

The key words in the admonition to the children are "obey" and "honor." For the fathers, it is "not to provoke." It's interesting that fathers and not mothers are asked to restrain from provoking their children. Since mothers have a physical bond with their children from the moment of conception, do they have more tenderness toward their children after carrying them for nine months in her womb?

When children obey and honor their parents, and fathers do not provoke their children to anger, all the three important elements of their relationships—trust, respect, and tough love—are present. When children understand that obeying and honoring their parents ensures their well-being and longevity, it is easier to accept tough love from their parents, especially their dads.

An Effective Conflict-Resolution Approach

Dozens of excellent books prescribe comprehensive and complex approaches, but the Bible offers a simple and effective solution to resolve family conflicts. As Abraham's and Lot's flocks began to multiply, conflicts arose between their respective herdsmen because the limited land was unable to support their growing needs.

Abraham's conflict-resolution approach was characterized by three basic elements:

1. acknowledgment
2. relational priorities
3. first choice for others

Acknowledgment

Abraham recognized there was a problem and promptly offered a mutually beneficial solution. He did not shove it under the rug. He said to Lot, "Please let there be no strife between you and me, and between my herdsmen and your herdsmen" (Genesis 13:8).

Relational Priorities

Abraham put his relationship ahead of HIS position. After all, being the uncle, he could have used his positional authority to delay the conflict-resolution step. Instead, he told Lot that "they shouldn't have any conflicts between themselves, because they are brethren" (Genesis 13:8).

First Choice for Others

Greed always contributes to poor conflict resolution. When we offer the first choice to the dissenting party, it's amazing how we are blessed despite what might seem like taking advantage of largeness of heart. Abraham gave the first choice to his nephew to select which part of the land he wanted to have. Lot selected the well-watered, fertile-looking plains of Jordan. In fact, the land "looked like the garden of the Lord ... And Abraham took the other part of the land which Lot did not choose—the land of Canaan (Genesis 13:9–12).

God blessed Abraham, but Lot had to be rescued by Abraham from Sodom and Gomorrah (Genesis 14:12–16). The main point of Abraham's approach to settling the conflict with Lot was that Abraham quickly acknowledged the problem, placed higher value on family relationships than property, and offered the first choice of selection—without any greed or exploitative intent. God honors such attitudes. Abraham is considered the father of all nations—Jewish, Christian, Muslim, and all others.

We see so many rifts in families because of property matters. If they are resolved the way Abraham did, we'll have more content, joyful families for generations to come. Otherwise, poisoned, resentful, bitter relationships are what we'll see.

The Power of Family Prayer

A family that prays together stays together. However, so many families have been falling apart because they don't pray as a family at least once a day. My wife, Chaya, tells us how her dad, as the spiritual head of the family, gathered his wife and six children every morning and evening after for family prayers. In my family, my mother convened family prayers with my sister and me. My dad eventually joined us. In my own family, Chaya and our sons and I had family prayers every night, usually before dinner.

There are many benefits of family prayers:

1. Family prayers represent a collective, communication with God—praising Him, thanking Him, and bringing intercessory requests to Him.
2. Family prayers teach the family to depend on God for everything and in all circumstances.
3. Family prayers provide comfort and strength when someone else in the family prays for them with empathy and love.

4. Family prayers create a transparent communication system among family members. If one family member has an important and urgent need (an important exam, an interview for a job, a contract on a house, or the death of a relative or friend), the whole family gets to know it and continues praying about it in the hours and days ahead.
5. Family prayers set an example to relatives and friends when they come for lunches, dinners, or special occasions.
6. Family prayers unify the family, especially during periods of adversity.
7. Family prayers provide perspective and contentment and have made a big difference in my family. Every benefit listed above has been realized by me during the past seventy-seven years.

There's a power about prayer in general, especially family prayer. Every spiritual leader in the Bible relied on prayer. Jesus spent much time in prayer, especially before critical decisions. He once prayed all night (Luke 6:12).

Paul and his spiritual associate Silas prayed all night and sang hymns after being beaten badly and imprisoned in Philippi. God let the chains drop like there was an earthquake. The jailer was scared to death that Paul and Silas would flee, but they didn't. On the contrary, Paul assured the jailer that they were very much there. The jailer was witnessed to by Paul's faith, and that night, the jailer's wife and family were transformed forever spiritually (Acts 16:25–34).

What about the dozens of miracles that happened because of the faithful, fervent prayers of men, women, and children? Daniel and his friends were rescued from the lion's den when they did not compromise their belief in God and prayed consistently (Daniel 6:18–23). Hannah prayed incessantly for a child, and God granted her request (1 Samuel 1:8–27). Peter, one of Jesus's inner-circle disciples, was imprisoned on the orders of King Herod in the first century AD, but constant prayers were offered to God for him by the church. An angel, appointed by God, visited Peter at night in the prison and made his chains fall off his hands. The angel led him out, and Peter went to the house of Mary, the mother of John Mark, and they were praying (Acts 12:1–24).

Does it mean that our prayers will always result in an outcome we expect? No. God answers our prayers one of three ways: "Yes," "no," or "not now." We need to truly yield to God's perfect will and say, "Lord, whatever you think should be done, please let that be done, and whatever your answer is, I want to bring glory and honor to you and to you alone." We'll experience the inner peace even when the answers are "no" or "not now." Just as steel gets hardened and tempered through repeated heating, beating, and cooling, God hardens us with spiritual stamina and strength by taking us through adversities and trials. In fact, He perfects us through them to become more like Him (James 1:2–4).

A richer life ensues when God enables us to show our mettle through tough circumstances because we can comfort and strengthen those who experience similar situations in their lives. We take so many things for granted. When we woke up this morning and brushed our teeth and took a shower, we probably never thought about how much of an ordeal it is for some people to do that because of their challenging physical or emotional conditions. If you are reading this right now, what a blessing you have. There are millions of blind people, including our nephew, who can't do that so easily.

Prayers provide a perspective in life for all the members of the family unit. They offer a sense of contentment for what they have already and what so many are deprived of so many basic functions of our bodies and minds. The prayers of hundreds from around the world helped when our younger son Paul suddenly went to be with Jesus on June 23, 2000. I have learned to be in prayerful state—I call it "SOP" (state of prayer)—to feel God's power to intercede for others rather than just for us. In fact, when we pray for others, our problems pale in comparison to theirs—and we don't feel that bad after all. If we practice just two spiritual disciplines daily—Bible reading and praying, we'll enjoy inner peace even in the toughest times.

The Meaningful Mealtimes

In the United States, family mealtimes have become rare during the past thirty years. Communication is taking place more through internet chats than through face-to face talks. A few years ago, I observed two employees sending emails to each other from their cubicles, which were just three feet apart. Today, children—even at the age of four—are using cyber chats more than face-to-face communication. In the 1990s, Faith Popcorn was predicting the "cocooning" phenomenon where people get isolated more and more to themselves. Unfortunately, as many people are not using technology in a relevant manner, we see more of islands of communication than families and communities of communication.

My sister and I learned so much about American history without even taking a course on it from the natural discussions during family mealtimes. We learned the basic etiquette of eating and communicating via this daily routine. As both husband and wife have been going to work—of necessity or by choice—family mealtimes have slowly disappeared. First, it was the family breakfast, and then it was the family dinners. In the past, eating was not considered a chore. It was a family communication time: good and bad and sad or joyous. Is it possible to return to these family mealtimes? Yes. How?

1. Consider family mealtimes a part of the daily routine. Whatever we consider important, we do it. Where there is a will, there is a way.

2. Start with one family mealtime first—either breakfast or dinner—whichever is more feasible in the beginning. Habits can't be changed overnight. Change, to be effective, must be gradual.

3. Agree to some ground rules during mealtimes. For example, come as soon as called. Have an attitude of gratitude. Do not bring up controversial issues. Each member of the family unit says a brief prayer. Have each person share something that's of interest to the family.

4. Do steps 2–3 for at least one month, and then it becomes a habit.
5. Add one more family mealtime. Two are pretty good. If you are retired, you and your spouse may have the luxury of all three mealtimes, including lunchtime.

The important thing about the family eating together is making these times meaningful by adding value spiritually, emotionally, intellectually, and socially. Family mealtimes are like the grease in the bearings. They make family unit operate smoothly and reduce friction daily. Spiritual and emotional friction, if not overcome daily, result in festering misunderstandings between husband and wife, parents and children, and siblings. A family that eats together will grow together, work together, play together, and share together.

The Bible is full of examples of communal mealtimes. Moses ate the family meals at the Passover. Mephibosheth (son of Saul) was treated like a family member by King David, and Mephibosheth sat at the dinner table with David. Jesus ate meals with His disciples. One of the most memorable and meaningful times was the night of the Passover—just before He went out with them to the Garden of Gethsemane and Judas Iscariot betrayed Him.

Family mealtimes accentuate and enhance the richness of relationships. In 2015, the Family Meals Movement was started as a campaign in the US, and in just one month, it grew exponentially. During the COVID-19 pandemic, families began to eat together more. This movement has grown to a point where September has become the National Family Meals Month. "The aim is simple: commit to staying strong with family meals." FMI.org presents more information, but a few salient highlights of FMI's research indicate several important things:

1. Regular family meals are linked to higher grades and self-esteem and delayed sexual activity among youth.
2. Children, used to family meals, show positive social behaviors as adults, such as sharing, fairness, and respect.

3. With each additional family meal, adolescents are less prone to violence, depression, and suicide and less likely to use or abuse drugs or run away.
4. Adults and children having more regular family meals are less likely to suffer from obesity.

Visit the website FMI.org to see some extremely positive results from a study reported in the *Journal of Adolescent Health*.

Three Actions I Can Take for One Month after Reading This Chapter

1.
2.
3.

Chapter Four
PLANNING

*Commit your work to the Lord, and your
thoughts will be established.*
—**PROVERBS 16:3**

*For I know the plans I have for you, declares the Lord, plans to
prosper you and not harm you, plans to give you hope and a future.*
—**JEREMIAH 29:11 (NIV)**

*Many are the plans in a person's heart, but it
is the Lord's purpose that prevails.*
—**PROVERBS 19:21 (NIV)**

*For which of you, intending to build a tower, does not sit down
first and count the cost, whether he has enough to finish it.*
—**LUKE 14:28**

Planning is the process of developing a plan. A plan is a blueprint of action for the future. Planning is always concerned with the why, what, where, when, who, and how of the future.

In enterprises, three types of planning are normally done. Long-term (strategic) planning is for a period usually greater than five years; medium-term planning is for periods of two to four years, and short-term planning is for periods up to one year. Each of these has different objectives. The important point to remember here is that family units need long-term, medium-term, and short-term planning because a family unit has many similarities with an enterprise (as detailed in chapter 2).

Long-Term (Strategic) Planning

This type of planning is characterized by long-term thinking, core values, core competencies, vision, mission, and goals, and effectiveness of goals.

Long-Term Thinking

For decades, enterprises that think about the long term have had success, including the American giants GE, GM, Ford, 3M, IBM, and AT&T; Japanese companies like Toyota, Matsushita, and SONY; German firms like Mercedes-Benz Group and Siemens; and Indian corporate houses like Tata, Birla, Shriram, Godrej, Mahindra, and Reliance. Similarly, family units that think about the long term will also have long-lasting positive impact on our society.

When we take pride in our family units and expect them to contribute to the world—in line with God's perfect will—we have taken the first step for preserving responsible and positive growth of our societies: spiritually, economically, emotionally, physically, and environmentally. There's strength, stability, and resilience with family units that think about the long term because they perpetuate their good family name and heritage. The Bible tells us that a "good name is better than great riches" (Proverbs 22:1).

Core Values

Core values represent fundamental beliefs. They are the pillars that support a vision, a mission, and goals that contribute to the common good. Core values enable enterprises to align their operational philosophies and implementation processes to accomplish their vision, mission, and goals without compromising on their basic beliefs and value systems.

Core values also enable an enterprise to reorient itself and rediscover itself when times are tough. IBM is a case in point. In the 1980s, IBM began to lose considerable market share. Its stock value plummeted from $160 a share to $40. Lou Gerstner had turned around Nabisco (a food manufacturer) and was hired to reestablish IBM's preeminence. After visiting thousands of IBM employees, Lou Gerstner realized that IBM was IBM because of its original core values: mutual respect, excellence, and customer focus. He revisited these core values, came up with his own fourteen principles, and turned around IBM in about a decade.

Family units also must define their core values and follow them to manage their families for many generations. When we distill God's wisdom for families and individuals from the Bible, we see many important core values a family can choose from (preferably all of them):

1. agape (sacrificial) love
2. character
3. compassion
4. contentment
5. equality/inclusion
6. fairness
7. faith
8. godly fear
9. inner joy
10. integrity
11. meekness

12. mercy
13. mutual respect
14. patience
15. peace
16. praise
17. prayer
18. unity (with diversity)

Whenever a family unit or its members faces problems or crises, it's almost always true that they have been ignoring one or more of these core values. For example, when a husband and wife are having constant arguments about a lack of money to buy and enjoy things like their neighbors, is it possible that they are not following the core values of faith, contentment, and patience? When family members are in a constant state of dissatisfaction with each other, is it possible that the core values of prayer, mutual respect, patience, and mercy have been ignored in recent days, weeks, or months?

God, the designer of the family unit, has the knowledge to fix things that go wrong in families. Unfortunately, we look for solutions outside God's "instruction manual." Wouldn't it make sense to read His manual (the Bible) and follow His instructions?

Core Competencies

Every family unit has its own set of core competencies. Core competencies are the unique and extraordinary intellectual, economic, social, and vocational strengths. Most families don't even know that this is the case. They simply dabble in every new flavor of the month.

When we try to do things outside the capabilities of our core competencies, we experience a lack of confidence, lack of interest, frustration, low success, and a low sense of fulfillment. This is why so many people go to work just to earn money to support their families. For them, work is simply an unavoidable inconvenience in their lives. They work because they have to and not because they want to. Those who recognize their core competencies consistently do things that align with such competencies, their work is interesting and enjoyable, and they have a proper perspective about work—even when there are challenges on a day-to-day basis with the boss, working conditions, or internal politics.

Many people take vocational detours in their lives to find that so-called perfect job. Ultimately, they retire without finding that perfect job. God has given us innate strengths and weaknesses. When we identify those special strengths based on our family histories, we can prayerfully develop a vision, mission, and a set of goals for our lives. We may achieve all of them fully, but just identifying them and following a systematic process of carrying through with them is a lot better than frustration and low sense of fulfillment.

On my mother's side, for nearly four generations, most men were engineers, teachers, or preachers. From my father's side, most men were teachers. On both sides of the family, the common core competency has been teaching. I recognized this core competency when I was thirty-three years old. Once I wrote my personal mission statement, based on my core competencies, my attitude and focus changed considerably. I have been enjoying teaching and writing for more than forty years now.

On My wife's side, many have been in service by preaching or teaching. For my children, we identified core competencies of teaching, preaching, and service. I advised my family not to go into business. We don't seem to be naturally wired for that. We can certainly try, but it'd be frustrating and less fulfilling than teaching, preaching, or humanity service.

The Bible talks about the twelve tribes of Israel: Asher, Benjamin, Dan, Gad, Issachar, Judah, Levi, Manasseh, Ephraim, Naphtali, Rueben, Simeon, and Zebulun. The Levi tribe was designated by God as priests (Numbers 16:5; 18:1, 8; Exodus 28:1). Priesthood was its primary core competency, designated by God Himself. King Saul, Israel's first monarch, from the tribe of Benjamin, offered sacrifices (a priestly duty, only to be done by a Levite priest), and when he ignored

Samuel's directive from God, the Lord got very angry and punished him (1 Samuel 12–15).

God, of course, knows our core competencies because He designed us. It is for us to identify them through prayer, introspection, and keen observation of the vocations of our ancestors.

Vision, Mission, and Goals

Vision

The Bible says, "When there is no vision, people perish" (Proverbs 29:18. KJV). What is a vision? A vision is a picture of the preferred future—far into time, usually ten, twenty, thirty, or even one hundred years. It is an idealistic, altruistic, and utopian visualization of the future. A vision should never be achievable. If it is, then it ceases to be a vision. From a practical standpoint, it is expressed through a vision statement.

Some examples of well-prepared corporate vision statements are given in table 4.1.

Table 4.1 Examples of Some Vision Statements

Organization	Vision Statement
Apple, Inc.	"We believe that we are on face of the earth, to make great products, and that's not changing." [2022]
Tesla, Inc.	"Create the most compelling car company of the 21st century by driving the world's transition to electric vehicles." [2023]
University of Miami	"We will strive to transform the world in positive ways through innovative education, impactful research and scholarship, and the translation of knowledge into solutions." [2023]
The Vatican City	"Working together with the Holy See, Embassy Vatican will continue to promote peace, freedom, and human rights throughout the world." [2022]
Toyota Company	Toyota will lead the future mobility society, enriching lives around the world with the safest and most responsible ways of moving people." [2021]
United Nations	"To reduce and eliminate extreme poverty, to ensure sustainability of economic and social development, to strengthen human dignity and rights and to prevent violent conflicts." [2021]
Oxford University	"To be a global center of excellence for lifelong learning." [2023]
Space X	"To revolutionize space technology with the ultimate goal of enabling people to live on other planets." [2023]

Joshua took over the mantle of leadership after Moses, and he articulated his personal vision very clearly almost 2,600 years ago: "As for me and my house, we shall serve the Lord" (Joshua 24:15). His vision was realized for many years after his death, but because of the nearly 1,900-year break in Israel's national identity as a country (AD 70 to May 14, 1948), it's hard to know exactly how long Joshua's vision statement was operative. I adopted the same vision statement as Joshua almost fifty years ago. For as long as I live, I want to remind my family unit that we should serve the one and only God the Bible points to.

Mission

A mission is the purpose for existence. A mission statement represents the mission of an individual, family, community, enterprise, or country. It asks the fundamental question: "What is your purpose?" That's why a mission statement is also called a *purpose statement*. It asks why an entity exists. Here are a few examples of effective mission statements:

1. Christ Fellowship Church, Palmetto Bay, Florida: "Impact the world with the love and message of Jesus Christ—everyone, every day, everywhere."
2. Calvary Chapel, Fort Lauderdale, Florida: "Connect people to God, connect people to people, and connect people to outreach."
3. The American Red Cross: "Prevent and alleviate human suffering in the face of emergencies by mobilizing the power of volunteers and the generosity of donors."

In the context of a family unit, a mission statement should be developed by each person in the family when that individual is in seventh grade or higher. If it is done too early, the mission statement would not last long because the child doesn't have a sufficient grasp of their core competencies, guiding values, strengths, and weaknesses.

From my experience with university engineering students, I find that many of them don't know what specialization they really must pursue after their degree is completed. We know from sociological studies that the period from twenty to twenty-four is crucial in the way young adults orient themselves for the next phase of life. Therefore, it is best to have youths write their personal mission statements at least one year before they enter college or university. This is a practical step to take since every university will ask for an essay as part of the application. A student who articulates a personal mission in the essay is bound to get noticed in a positive way.

I spent nearly six months in prayer, introspection, and assessment of my family's core competencies (teaching, preaching, and service), my personal guiding values (integrity, loyalty, dependability), my intellectual and analytical strengths (twelve years of engineering education and six years of industrial experience), and my weaknesses (impatience). I wrote my personal mission statement as I was completing my doctoral studies in Chicago in 1979: "I want to help improve the standard of living of people around the world.

The standard of living of a country and its labor productivity are very closely related—with more than 80 percent correlation. Since my doctoral work was in developing productivity measurement models, I thought about being a professor in a university. I could teach about the importance of measurement and improvement approaches to productivity in several countries and help them improve their standard of living. I have a long way to go, but as of 2023, I have been able to teach about productivity in more than fifty countries, and through my writings, I have influenced many more, improving their productivity, standard of living, and quality of work life.

In 2001, after the tragic death of our youngest son, Paul, I spent many months reexamining my first personal mission statement of 1979 and taking into account the new spiritual strengths I found: faith and trust in God to hold me and my family even through the valley of death, a deep conviction of hope to see my son again, and an unconditional love that so many people in the world do not experience. This hope made me revise my personal mission statement on January 1, 2000: "To serve God with trust, obedience, and praise."

I continue to teach at the same university I have been at since 1979, but this new mission statement has been propelling me into newer realms that I never imagined before. A major reason for writing this book is to accomplish my new mission statement in life for as long as God has earmarked me for.

In summary, the way families operate in the future can significantly improve if they spend time prayerfully and thoughtfully in developing a vision statement for their family units and encouraging their family members to develop personal mission statements. This exercise can go a long way toward motivating each other toward family goals.

Goals

Goals are tangible and intangible objectives for accomplishing the mission of an individual, family, community, enterprise, or country. Thus, every family member who develops a mission statement should list a set of goals that, when accomplished, will move the person closer to achieving their mission statement.

Setting goals is ideally done on an annual basis. It may take a few hours or a few days to share the goals with the family members at the dawn of the new year.

We, the Sumanth family, have been following a tradition since our children were in elementary school. On New Year's Eve, we list our goals, share them with each other, and enter the new year with a prayer, asking God to help us achieve our new goals. We try to be diligent by listing our goals in three categories: spiritual, personal, and professional (table 4.2). Of course, our children and grands may not always be 100 percent diligent.

Table 4.2 An Example of My Goals

Goals for Jan 1–December 31, 2023

Spiritual Goals
1. Read my Bible 3 times a day (morning, evening, and night).
2. Pray daily for everyone who is listed in the Week's Prayer Requests.
3. Pray for my family members throughout the day, by being in a state of prayer (SOP).
4. Teach the Bible Study class about every 5 weeks.
Personal Goals
1. Have a refreshing, one-week trip with my wife and 3 family friends to Washington, DC, Niagara Falls, and visit close friends in Toronto.
2. Have a family vacation for a week, if possible, to the Caribbean or Europe.
Professional Goals:
1. Complete my manuscript on Family By the Bible™.
2. Sign a contract with a publisher for this book.
3. Take a "compassion Trip" to the South Asia, touching the lives of the poor and destitute children through education, motivation, and prayer.
4. Lecture at one to two universities to MBA and Ph.D. students.

Each goal can only be considered a goal if it satisfies the following five criteria:

1. It must help achieve the mission statement.
2. It must be practically feasible.
3. It must be specific.
4. It must be a time-based.
5. It must be verifiable.

For example, in the spiritual category, we see that the spiritual goals, when achieved, would help accomplish my personal mission statement. These are practically feasible, specific, time-based, and verifiable (or measurable) goals.

Effectiveness of Setting Goals

In each category of goals, we can determine what I call the "effectiveness index," which represents the extent to which the goals have been accomplished. For example, in 2023, if I accomplish three of the four spiritual goals, my effectiveness index will be 75 percent. The maximum score is 100 percent in each category of goals (spiritual, personal, and professional).

Goals that cannot be achieved in one particular year could be added to the next year's list (if appropriate). Don't get discouraged by the effectiveness index. Even when it is low, you are in a much better position than most others who have no idea about what they want to do with their lives without a vision, mission, and goals. As you get into the habit of making the goal list every year, you'll get better at the process.

The goals are set annually, but the mission statement doesn't get revised every year. If it must be revised too often, it was not prepared carefully enough. My first mission statement lasted twenty-two years (1979–2001), and my second one is still relevant after nearly twenty-two years (2001–Present). Of course, your vision statement shouldn't change for at least forty years (one generation) if at all. A vision is something that may never be achieved because it's an ideal, altruistic situation, but moving toward its achievement results in so much good when compared to operating without a vision, mission, and goals.

Medium-Range Planning

Families have many situations and events in the two-to-four-year range of planning time. We'll discuss the three very important things families must plan in the medium range:

- o   raising a family
- o   going on family vacations

o planning special events (birthdays, anniversaries, family reunions)

Raising a Family

A major part of planning in a family is planning for children shortly after marriage.

Planning for Children

Parents first plan for children and then for their education. It is increasingly common for newly marrieds to wait at least two or three years before having their first child. Well, is this is a smart thing to do? First, according to the Bible, "Behold, children are a heritage from the Lord" (Psalm 127:3). The NIV uses "gift" for "heritage." Does the Gift-giver choose the time to offer a gift? Do the recipients have any say in it? What are the fundamental reasons for choosing a "convenient" time to raise a family? Clearly, God, as the Gift-giver of children, chooses His timing, and no matter what a couple thinks about planning, it's going to happen anyway. Why not put everything in God's hands and pray from day one after marriage that His will be done?

The most common reasons young couples offer for postponing having children for a few years include the following:

1. time to get to know each other
2. time to finish education (if still pursuing education)
3. time to save up a bit more

All these and other reasons could be quite reasonable, but this perspective is missing a lack of trust and faith in God to provide for everything.

My parents—and others for thousands of years—never did the kind of planning this generation does when it comes to having children. When we completely trust in God, His sovereignty, and His ability to provide in all circumstances, we let Him do things according to His plan and not ours. Chaya and I had our first child as a doctoral student with a stipend, of about three hundred dollars per month. On top of that, it was a high-risk pregnancy.

God provided for all our expenses before, during, and after the pregnancy. My professor offered some opportunities for additional income. I worked another extra job, and we had enough to cover all our expenses. We even saved some money. I consider a child a biological bond between husband and wife. When times are tough, it's even more of a reason not to postpone having a child. During my doctoral work, which tests one's patience every day, there were many times when I'd come home dejected because of the pressure of so many things. As soon as I stepped into my student apartment, and our little Johnny came running for me, saying "Daddy, Daddy," I forgot about all the day's challenges.

Don't try to manipulate God's plan for you. Instead, simply yield to His plan, which is always perfect. If we truly believe that "all things work together for good to those who love God, to those are the called according to His purpose" (Romans 8:28), we'll stop tampering with God's perfect plans and start yielding to Him.

Planning for Education

After planning for children, parents need to plan for their education. I see parents getting so concerned about their children's education, especially their college education, that they become almost paranoid. While some college planning is reasonable and necessary, parents do not need to stress about college planning. Instead of stressing out around the tenth grade, parents can start motivating them in kindergarten and first grade and explaining the importance of education for life, learning and practicing effective study habits, and pursuing their personal mission statements with commitment, enthusiasm, and consistency.

That's what my parents did. My sister and I did exceptionally well academically from first grade. My parents never had to pay a penny for our college degrees. Today, a typical private university in the United States charges between $100,000 and $300,000 for a four-year baccalaureate degree, and most parents must take out large loans. Imagine the financial burden if there are two or more children.

Increasingly, a master's degree is becoming a necessity, particularly in professions such as engineering, business, and law. Imagine the huge amount of money parents must set aside. Instead, maybe parents are better off giving a fraction of that as a wedding gift and/or a down payment for a small house.

Parents must inspire their children to focus on education, be fiercely competitive in a positive way in their classes, and keep their priorities right in school. Higher education offers opportunities to learn critical thinking, creative problem-solving, presentation skills, networking with and making friends from around the world, and exposure to national and international thought leaders.

During my undergraduate engineering program (1962–1967), my mother said, "Son, keep your priorities on your education until you graduate. Don't think of girls for the next five years, and I'll be looking for a suitable girl for you." Once I finished my baccalaureate degree and started working, she said "Well, now, son, it is OK for you to be looking out for the girl you want to marry." About four years later, I told my mother about the girl I wanted to marry. She blessed my choice. Neither of our two boys had to pay a penny for their college educations either. My wife and I basically did what my parents did. This system worked for us.

When parents give their children the "right" tools for college (inspiration, motivation, passion, good study habits, and supportive environment), that's more important than simply saving hundreds of thousands of dollars for their education when children take their parents' sacrifices for granted instead of being self-motivated and self-sacrificial. This approach builds character, a spirit of self-reliance, stewardship, and excellent work ethic—traits every young adult needs in adulthood.

Planning for Children's Weddings

Once the children graduate and start earning wages, their parents start planning their weddings. Weddings are one-day events in most Western cultures. In some Eastern cultures, wedding ceremonies may last two to seven days. They certainly need much more planning. Being an exciting time for everyone, weddings are the one time when opportunities for mishaps in communication (see chapter 3) abound, credit card debt can mount, tempers can flare, and a host of other unexpected things can happen. What can you do? Not too much—but certainly something. You cannot eliminate the pain of such events, but you can minimize the pain. Perhaps it's better to offer general principles here than specific suggestions.

Involvement

Involve your immediate family, extended family, close relatives, and friends in the planning process for the wedding, especially if it's the first one. In Western cultures, most wedding activities are planned by the couples. In Eastern cultures, parents do the planning for the most part. Therefore, there is a smaller probability that someone or something important will be left out. If mistakes are made in planning and execution, damage control to patch up misunderstandings later is neither easy nor fun.

Cooperation and Not Complaining

It is so easy for close relatives or family members to expect to be pampered even when a zillion little things still need to be done. It means so much more to the overall beauty of the wedding when people are pitching in and helping without being asked.

Never Running Out

The worst thing that can happen is running out of food, drinks, or anything else. After spending tons of money, it's not worth hearing nasty or sarcastic remarks about the shortages. It's best to have enough of everything.

Individual Attention

One can never give too much individual attention to guests. It's a cardinal mistake to ignore some while over-attending to others.

Planning for Retirement

Is retirement a biblical concept or a cultural concept? The only mention of age-based retirement in the Bible is in Numbers 8:25. The Levites, living off the tithes and offerings of their fellow Israelites, retired at age fifty as per God's directive. Being a cultural concept, however, most people want to retire and want to plan for it. The time to plan for retirement is not when the couple is just a few years before retirement. It must be addressed as early as within two years after marriage.

Three fundamental questions must be addressed regarding retirement:

1. If and when should I retire?
2. Where should I spend my retirement years?
3. What should I do upon retirement?

If and When Should I Retire?

The average retirement age in the thirty-four countries of the Organization for Economic Cooperation and Development (OECD) in 2014 was 65.0 for males and 63.5 for females. However, there's been a tendency to increase the retirement age as life expectancies rise.

The answer to this question depends upon the type of job you have. If you are a government employee in a Western country, like the United States, you may have to retire at sixty-five. If you're in a state government position in India, you may retire at fifty-eight. Generally, if you are working for a private university in the US, there's no retirement age. Some of my colleagues are well over seventy and are still active. If you own a business, you may probably retire partially at first and then fully after handing over your business to a person you have confidence in.

If you must retire at fifty-eight, sixty-two, sixty-five, or seventy, the important thing to remember is to keep yourself busy by contributing locally, nationally, and/or globally. In the Bible, kings generally maintained their positions until death. Disciples and apostles, such as Peter, Paul, and James, served God until they were martyred.

Studies show that those who retire and adopt a sedentary lifestyle die rather early, sometimes within seven or eight years. Those who keep themselves busy after retirement tend to enjoy a good quality of life. One of my colleagues took an early retirement at sixty-three and kept himself busy with community service and church activities. He died in his nineties, serving until the end. My grandfather, after his retirement at fifty-eight, opened his own Christian printing business and ran it almost until his last days when he was eighty-five.

Where Should I Spend My Retirement Years?

The answer to this important question depends upon many factors, including the following:

1. proximity to children and grandchildren
2. health
3. attachment to the last home where many memories have been made
4. proximity to friends and/or relatives

Until fifty years ago, most people retired and stayed wherever they grew up. Today, because of the dispersion of their children—in some cases, all over the world—the choice of location is not as easy.

The bottom line comes down to where you feel most comfortable spending your golden years. One of our good church friends was widowed about forty years ago. At eight-five, after a knee replacement, he was as active as a fifty-year-old. He lived in Miami-Dade County most of his life, but his second daughter insisted on him spending the rest of his life with her family near Washington DC. He moved there and lived happily there until his nineties.

Sometimes, there is no easy choice about where to spend retirement. Jacob, the father of the twelve tribes of Israel, had to travel to Egypt because there was a severe famine in Canaan. Joseph—the son who was sold by his brothers to an Egyptian was the second highest in authority next only to Pharaoh—and wanted to take care of his father, brothers, and their families.

After Pharaoh died, the Israelites were treated cruelly, and after almost 430 years, Moses led them out of Egypt. Jacob's bones were brought to the Promised Land, and he spent much of his retirement life in Egypt (Genesis 46–50). Jacob's final years were sovereignly determined by God. Ultimately, we should let God decide where we'll spend our golden years. Fortunately, technology enables us to feel connected to our dear ones despite thousands of miles separating us.

What Should I Do upon Retirement?

Those who keep themselves busy in their communities live fulfilled lives. The former president of the United States, Jimmy Carter, worked with Habitat for Humanity and built homes for those who couldn't afford them. He served as president from 1977 until 1981. He has kept himself busy until his nineties, going as an envoy to countries and representing the United States. He has been more in the spotlight after his presidency than before. He was awarded the 2002 Nobel Peace Prize for his work finding peaceful solutions to international conflicts, advancing democracy and human rights, and promoting economic and social development.

According to the United Nations, life expectancies have risen steadily around the world since 1955: 75.6 years for females, 70.8 for men, and 73.2 combined. The highest combined life expectancies in 2023 are for Hong Kong 85.29, Japan 85.03, Switzerland 84.25, Singapore 84.07, Germany 81.58, UK 81.77, the United States 79.11, and India 70.42. Nigeria is 55.75.

The average life expectancy for women in the United States is 81.65, and it is 76.61 for men. Therefore, after retiring at sixty-five, there are still eleven to seventeen years left. Finding something useful to do is a matter of necessity. Health care costs in the US have been so high that many older retirees have had to work part-time to keep up with inflation, health care premiums, and prescription medicines.

Many volunteer services need older men and women to supplement their paid employees. Working at such places is emotionally rewarding. I know a gentleman in his eighties who's a mentor to a student in the business school.

The Bible talks about older women being mentors to younger ones. Women's Bible study groups are a great example of older women encouraging, counseling, and imparting their wisdom to younger women with little children. The same is true with men.

Wisdom comes with life experiences. It's only natural that retired men and women offer their sage counsel to whoever needs it. In many ancient cultures, the older you are, the greater the respect you are given for your knowledge, wisdom, and life experiences. We need to rediscover the merit of this thinking in the Western world.

Planning Family Vacations

Family vacations are supposed to be fun and relaxing, but they often end up being stressful, boring, or bad. Family vacations have many benefits:

1. They create an environment where every family member helps make minor or major decisions.
2. They offer an opportunity for teamwork, focusing on the same goals, and having a good time in an enjoyable and safe manner.
3. They build stronger relationships within the family.

Plan the tasks before, during, and after the vacation:

1. Assign tasks to family members.
2. Plan for sufficient time between events.
3. Have contingency plans. If plan A doesn't work, try plan B or C.
4. Understand the real reason for taking the family vacation by occasionally reminding each other of it.
5. Show enthusiasm—especially when Dad and Mom are around. Otherwise, they might feel hurt after spending all that money.
6. Demonstrate mutual respect in public and in private.
7. Show an accommodative spirit when and wherever it is needed.
8. Have a common understanding of the things not to do.

With the simple application of these principles, your family vacations can be fun.

Planning Special Events

Celebrating special events like birthdays and anniversaries are effective ways to create strong, long-lasting, and example-setting relationships in a family unit. Two basic approaches for recognizing special events are predictable and unpredictable.

It is better to have predictable celebrations than no celebrations. My wife is a queen of surprises. She surprised me on my fortieth, fiftieth, sixtieth, and seventieth birthdays. She was really surprised that I planned our twenty-fifth wedding anniversary. God willing, our fiftieth wedding anniversary in 2024 will be a blessing to us and our families and friends. For fifty years, we've celebrated every birthday and anniversary in our family unit. There's something very special about that.

Other special events we celebrate together as a family are New Year's Day, Valentine's Day, Easter, Thanksgiving, and Christmas. Every one of these events is an opportunity to get together, bond together, talk about our recent experiences, reminisce about old memories, and be together as a family.

The Bible talks about a number of festivals and special events the Jewish people celebrated—as directed by God. Many Orthodox Jews still celebrate these today. Not surprisingly, these families are very closely knit.

Short-Term Planning

All activities of less than one-year duration come under short-term planning. There are many items for which planning is important in family units. A few examples of such activities include the following:

1. weekday activities
2. weekend activities
3. spring cleaning and garage sales

Weekday Activities

Many weekday activities, when planned well, can be done effectively and efficiently and with little physical or emotional stress. These include everything from cleaning, cooking, washing, drying, eating, resting, and walking. Each family unit has its own routines and priorities for daily activities, but some principles can help accomplish these more productively:

1. Plan the tasks at least a day before in your mind or on a notepad.
2. Plan for consistency rather than for being sporadic or impulsive.
3. Plan for short breaks whenever feasible (even if they are just ten or fifteen minutes).
4. Plan for a relatively even pace of work instead of too much variation during the day.
5. Plan to drink plenty of water throughout the day (even if it entails going to the restroom more than you wish to).

Weekend activities

In Western countries, weekends are Friday through Sunday; other countries usually have two days off every week. In the West, Fridays are generally for family nights out, Saturdays are for chores and going to temple (if Jewish), and Sundays are for church and relaxation at home.

In America, restaurants tend to be open for most of the day on weekends. Twenty-four-hour ATMs, restaurants, and pharmacies are both positive and negative. They are positive for convenience, but they are negative for the moneymaking mindset of the vendors.

The Bible tells us that God instructs us to keep the Sabbath holy. For Jews, it is Saturday; for Christians, it is Sunday. When we make the Sabbath a "day of convenience," we are disrespecting God's wisdom. There needs to be a balance in our lives. Try to plan your weekends with that in mind.

Spring Cleaning and Garage Sales

In the United States, spring cleaning usually happens in March or April. During this time, we try to get rid of as much junk as possible by giving it away to Goodwill or the Salvation Army or selling it in a garage sale. Many single-family homes and townhomes have two-car garages, but most of them only park one car. The other space is filled up with stuff.

When most people have more space, they collect more things—whether they really need them or not. A good short-term strategy is to get rid of all the unneeded things so that we waste less space, save money, and own things instead of them owning us.

In my family and my son's family, we have a simple principle to prevent accumulating unneeded stuff. We always keep the two spaces in the garage for our cars. At the end of the day, both cars must be parked inside the garage. This way, if we are buying and acquiring more things than we need, they'll start cluttering the bedrooms, family room, and living room. If we notice clutter, we get rid of it. We have learned not to buy too many things, and if we do, we give something away to charitable organizations every four or six months.

With spring cleaning and garage sales, it's a good idea to make a checklist of tasks as part of the planning. This cuts down on wasted time, effort, and energy.

Chapter Summary

1. It is important for family units to do long-term planning, medium-term planning, and short-term planning.
2. As part of long-term planning, a family unit should identify its core competencies and core values and develop a vision statement, mission (purpose) statement, and set spiritual, personal, and professional goals.
3. On the last day of each year, the family unit should sit down together, evaluate the effectiveness of their goals, and start the new year with a new set of goals. Beginning the new year

as a family unit recalling the blessings of the year and asking for the prayers of each other is great.

Three Actions I Can Take for One Month after Reading This Chapter

1.
2.
3.

Chapter Five
ORGANIZING

Let all things be done decently and in order.
—1 CORINTHIANS 14:40

Just as an enterprise requires a clearly defined organizational structure, a family unit also needs a well-defined and clearly understood organizational form. In enterprises, the organizational form is represented by an organization chart (figure 5.1).

Fig. 5.1 A Typical Organizational Structure up to Second Level in an Enterprise

Creating the Structure for Family Legacy and Success

An organization chart for your family unit can only be as useful as the way you define and create your family success. What is family legacy and success? It's the extent to which a family unit is obedient to God in accomplishing what He wants the family to do, according to His perfect will.

Thus, family success occurs only when the family unit is doing what God wants it to do, and being obedient to His instructions. Understanding this concept of family success requires the family to constantly seek God's perfect plan for it and constantly be aware of God's instructions through His Word. It also requires family members to follow God's instructions. All of this implies obedience. That's the bottom line. To be successful, a family unit must be obedient to God in all God asks it to do.

Consider the family unit of Lot, Abraham's nephew, in Genesis 19. When God's angels asked Lot to flee Sodom and Gomorrah, the cities that were going to be destroyed because of their wickedness, the instruction to Lot's family was not to look behind. Lot's wife, out of curiosity, turned back to see the destruction and became a pillar of salt. Lot lost his wife, and his daughters lost their mother. To propagate his genes, they got him drunk and slept with him.

In contrast, consider Abraham's situation. When Abraham and his wife, Sarah, didn't have children, Sarah preempted God's blessing, did not wait for God's promise to be fulfilled, and asked Abraham to sleep with Hagar, his maid. Ishmael was born from this union, but God's plan eventually was fulfilled when Sarah gave birth to Isaac at a very old age. After Isaac grew to be a young man, God tested Abraham by asking Him to make a sacrifice. Abraham obeyed God despite the unimaginable pain. As he was about to sacrifice Isaac, God's angel told him to stop and blessed him with a covenant (Genesis 20–21).

In the above cases, one family unit was not so obedient—and the other was very obedient. Obedience doesn't just happen. It requires faith in God and in His Word. "Faith is the substance of things hoped for, the evidence of things not seen" (Hebrews 11:1). Faith requires believing in something God says He will do—even if you can't see it happening. A successful family unit consistently demonstrates faith.

A wisely designed building requires a strong foundation, environmental compliance, sustainability, and emotional positivity. The foundation, pillars, beams, trusses, and other components must be designed to withstand physical forces, stresses, and strains. When we want a family unit to be successful and sustainable, it must withstand the physical forces, stresses, and strains and spiritual, emotional, and financial forces. It's a challenging and continuous task.

How do we build a strong and sustainable family structure? Many components constitute a robust family:

1. a father who is the spiritual head and an administrative leader
2. a mother who is the harmonizer and home engineer.
3. children who honor their father, mother, and grandparents, and respect others
4. commitment to the institution of marriage
5. understanding the concept that everyone in the family has equal importance but different roles and responsibilities
6. the bond of perfection (agape/sacrificial love)

A schematic illustration of the structure for family success is shown in figure 5.2.

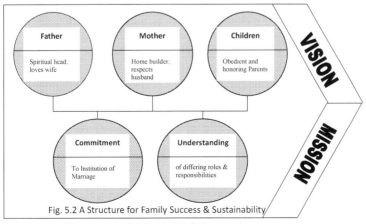

Fig. 5.2 A Structure for Family Success & Sustainability

A successful and sustainable family depends upon the extent to which these six components come together at any given time.

Commitment to the Institution of Marriage

Love is not shown separately in this structure. Agape love encompasses all five factors. Further, it grows with time in a family—out of commitment to the institution of marriage. Marriage is a sacred idea that God came up with. Adam and Eve were the first husband and wife. When God brought them together, His intention was that "a man shall leave his father and mother and be joined to his wife, and they shall become one flesh" (Genesis 2:24). Jesus said, "What God has joined together let no man separate" (Genesis 19:6; Mark 10:9).

The Five Fundamental Tenets of Marriage

Commitment to marriage creates certain common values in a family:

1. God hates divorce—and there's a price to pay for it.
2. A wedding is one day of excitement; marriage is a continual improvement process.
3. Marriage is three-part relationship for God, husband, and wife.
4. Family is God's organizational unit—It brings civility, nobility, and humanity to the world.
5. Every family unit is a laboratory on earth to discover God's greatness in the universe.

God Hates Divorce—and There's a Price to Pay for It

The Bible clearly points out that God hates divorce: "I hate divorce" (Malachi 2:16). After all, no designer likes to see their idea ridiculed. When husband and wife divorce, they are insulting God's idea of marriage.

Divorce was a social taboo when I was growing up fifty years ago. Today, the divorce date is a staggering 50 percent in the United States. With the ease with which a divorce can be obtained today, including no-fault divorces, a husband and wife find it easier than ever to simply forget the oath they took: "For better or worse until death do us part." Two people who said, "I can never live without you" during their courtship can suddenly declare, "We're not compatible for each other anymore" a year or two later?

When a couple divorces, they think they are going to eliminate a problem and go on to another relationship. This is far from the truth. There's always a price to pay for hasty decisions. This statement may sound cliché, but the brutally honest fact is that it is a "natural law." We cannot avoid it. The consequences of a divorce can be even more serious with children.

God allows divorce only under two conditions:

1. when there has been repeated, unrepentant infidelity on the part of the husband or wife
2. when the yoke is uneven (a believer marries an unbeliever and the unbeliever wants out)

The first situation can be prevented if the couple is committed to the sanctity and commitment to their wedding vow, if the husband loves his wife, and if the wife respects her husband. Prevention is always better than cure.

The second situation can be also avoided if the couple uses discretion. After all, marriage is like a welded joint of two metals. When you weld pieces of the same metal, it's easy, but if you weld different types of metals, it's more challenging.

Even those married for thirty, forty, or fifty years will tell you that they still don't completely understand their spouses. After all, when there are so many spiritual, cultural, educational, occupational, emotional, physical, and genetic differences to deal with, how can they be expected to? The commitment to discover each other is the exciting part of marriage, and many couples will tell you that.

Patience is needed, and it will come automatically when couples take their commitments to each other seriously. It is better to have minor problems while married than to have major problems while divorced.

A Wedding Is One Day of Excitement—Marriage Is a Continual Improvement Process

Realizing the differences between a wedding and marriage can help a marriage work. A wedding is the starting point of marriage. It's the beginning of a commitment to love and cherish each other for life. The beautiful moments will be captured and reminisced about many times thereafter.

Marriage, on the other hand, is an arduous journey of unexpected events—some good, some not so good—romance and intimate physical expressions, raising children and seeing their dreams come true, serving the community, adding positive value to society, seeing deaths in family and friends, and seeing a spouse widowed or a child dying. Marriage is a "school of hard knocks," but that's what makes it an institution. The experiences can be inspiring and instructional or challenging.

Marriage Is a Three-Part Relationship: God, Husband, and Wife

When God designed marriage, He knew it takes two to manage the family—both husband and wife. Even with both, it can seem overwhelming to attend to so many needs, especially during the transition points: a child's first day of kindergarten, graduation from high school, admission to college or university, weddings, retirement, and death. A husband and wife with opposite qualities often complement well each other. If one is hasty, the other is patient; if one is too careful with money, the other tends to be more extravagant; if one is impulsive, the other more tends to be deliberate; and if one feels hot, the other feels cold. God seems to deliberately pair husbands and wives together to complete each other and add to each other's knowledge and skills. There's no redundancy in marriage as God designed it.

God knows that a husband and wife are not sufficient to make a marriage successful. God knows that they both need to depend on Him. Thus, marriage is a three-way relationship for husband, wife, and God (figure 5.3).

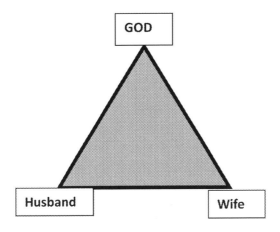

Fig 5.3 The Tripartite Relationship in Marriage

If a couple starts the day after their wedding by remembering this concept in figure 5.3, it will make a major difference in their married life. The husband and wife must keep their relationship with God as much as between themselves. As the husband and wife draw closer to God, they draw closer to each other too. When husband and wife realize that their marriage is enriching their relationship and their relationship with God, it makes a huge difference in the way they journey together. For years, they will enjoy their marriage instead of trudging along.

Imagine sitting on a stool with two equally spaced legs. It would be unstable. If you make the stool with three equally spaced legs, there is stability. A marriage of relationship of God, husband, and wife is strong and stable.

Family Is God's Organizational Unit

Discipline, work ethic, respect for others, honesty, integrity, and all other good values are taught in a family. Relational sensitivities are learned and practiced. A society whose citizens are indifferent, insensitive, uncivilized, and ignoble becomes an uncaring, arrogant society.

Today's telecommunication and internet systems have enabled people to do business globally and have a greater understanding of other cultures. It is all the more important that our kids are taught at home about the richness of diversity in cultures and how they should respect their customs without compromising their core values.

A family unit brings civility, nobility, and humanity to the world. Unfortunately, we have lost much of the civility, nobility, etiquette, and politeness during the past decade. We learned these positive traits from our parents, grandparents, uncles, and aunts. Today, because of broken family units, many kids grow up without proper guidance. Much damage has already been done. If we let one more generation lose the fundamental qualities of a civilized society, we can expect a much worse situation.

Every Family Unit Is a Laboratory on Earth to Discover God's Greatness in the Universe

A laboratory is a place for observations, discoveries, learning, and admiration. Likewise, a family unit is a place for discovering God's greatness in terms of His genius in creating a life and nurturing it through a family's spiritual, educational, financial, and physical support mechanism.

We learn so many things from our families' rich heritages. Families that keep their genealogies in written form pass on so much value to the following generations. We get confidence, self-esteem, and affirmation of our own personalities when we know our ancestors had similar traits. As we trace our ancestral families, we realize that we are special. God created us in His own image

(Genesis 1:27), and He loves us deeply (John 3:16). As we attempt to understand the universe He created, it is mind-boggling. We appreciate God' greatness even more because He cares for each of us individually, and He would like to have a close relationship with each one of us.

Results of a Poor Family Structure for Years to Come

The Bible summarizes the result of a poor family structure in one short phrase: "spiritual bondage." Spiritual bondage means being held back from discovering the truth about life, existence, and purpose. In a family that does not seek the ultimate truth, there is confusion, tension, low self-image, lack of purpose and direction, and a lack of assurance and stability. A family structure where the father and the mother have discovered this ultimate truth in God can perpetuate this mindset in its children for generations to come. This is a truly sustainable family.

Benefits of a Good Family Structure for Eternity

The Bible points out many benefits of a Christian family organization:

1. blessedness
2. anointing of the Holy Spirit
3. access to God and His power
4. delight in God
5. family sustainability
6. joy and inner peace
7. inheritance in eternal life
8. family harmony
9. confidence to go through tough times (including suffering)

A family that is structured to honor God glorifies Him and pleases Him and enables its members to receive so many benefits. What a privilege.

Three Actions I Can Take for One Month after Reading This Chapter

1.
2.
3.

Chapter Six
MOTIVATION

And whatever you do, do it heartily, as to the Lord and not to men.
—COLOSSIANS 3:23

Peple often say, "My children don't do a single thing around the house" or "My spouse doesn't care anything about the house." These are symptoms of a dysfunctional family that's lacking in motivation.

The Two Types of Motivation

The two types of motivation are *intrinsic motivation* and *extrinsic motivation*. Intrinsic motivation is the inner drive or desire to do things, accomplish tasks, achieve goals, and be a productive member of a family. Everyone has a certain level of intrinsic motivation. The key is to provide an atmosphere where such motivation comes to surface and thrives.

An employee at a Dutch electric utility company I was consultant for was a constant source of complaints from Human Resources. The problem was not the employee; it was the department head who was not identifying the employee's intrinsic motivation. This employee enjoyed working with computers in a creative manner, but she was given mundane clerical assignments. Once she was moved to a new assignment that used computers, her intrinsic motivation kicked in—and she became one of the most admired workers there.

God wired us up with intrinsic motivation for doing certain things that become our core competencies over time (see chapter 4). Extrinsic motivation is something that is imparted to us from our external environment. A nice office space with a lake view might be an extrinsic motivational factor that makes someone work with greater enthusiasm. The additional safety mechanisms installed in equipment for personal safety is another example of extrinsic motivation.

An effective family depends to a great extent upon its motivational mechanism. The absence of motivation in the family leads to a lack of a higher purpose for the family, poor communication and relationships between family members, a lack of enthusiastic participation in family matters, and a lack of common goals and direction for the family.

In the early literature on motivation, an abundance of theories includes those of Abraham Maslow (1943), Frederick Herzberg (1959), Douglas McGregor (1960), Victor Vroom (1964), L. W. Porter and Edward Lawler (1968), McClelland (1971), B. F. Skinner (1971), William Ouchi (1981), Edward Lawler (1982), and Ryan and Edward Deci (1985). These theories have had major benefits of motivating people in general.

For more than fifty years, I have applied my own motivation model, which I call the CEP Model. This model is practical and effective. It's not written up like the above-mentioned famous models, but it is based on fundamental assumptions about human beings as seen through God's loving eyes in the Bible.

The CEP Model of Motivation

This model (figure 6.1) recognizes three essential elements: caring (C), expectation (E), and positive reinforcement (P). Each of these must occur in order for motivation to be most effective. I acknowledge the impact of the above-mentioned theories in formulating my own CEP model, and I'm grateful for their basic elements of expectancy, and reinforcement, in particular. Though I have a detailed discussion of the above in my lectures, I must go straight to the CEP because of the length of this book.

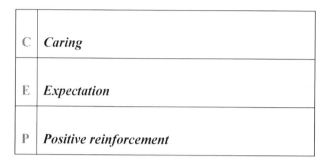

C	*Caring*
E	*Expectation*
P	*Positive reinforcement*

Fig 6:1 Sumanth's CEP Model of Motivation

Step 1: Caring

A caring atmosphere is the first condition for powerful, sustaining, and people-building motivation because people don't care how much you know until they know how much you care.

A genuinely caring environment shows you're not being exploitative of others. People resent it when they sense that they're being used or taken advantage of. This is especially true if they feel they've been ignored after putting their heart, soul, and mind into a task.

A genuinely caring environment indicates that you value others' welfare and security (emotional, physical, financial). You remember the help you received before, and you don't ignore them the next time they're passing by. Even if you're talking to someone else, you'll at least smile, make eye contact, or say hello.

A genuinely caring environment shows that you have integrity. If you promised to do something on a particular job or project, you keep the promise and do not replace the promise with a cheaper alternative. A genuinely caring environment also reinforces that you're not selfish and that you don't have a personal agenda. When you're caring, you understand the Bible's Golden Rule: "Do unto others, as you would like them to do unto you" (Matthew 7:12). This biblical principle was taught by Jesus.

Caring Is Genuine, Empathetic Love

The first-century disciples of Jesus were caring like Him, especially apostle Paul. His epistles to the churches in Corinth, Galatia, Ephesus, Macedonia, and Colossae showed his caring mindset. Mother Teresa epitomized this caring attitude. Her genuine, empathetic service to the lepers of Calcutta and her Missionaries of Charity, established in 1950, is active in 133 countries and provides dignity, love, and care to thousands of human beings.

People are hurting everywhere. It's not just the lepers, beggars, or the economically poor. It includes CEOs, celebrities, tough-looking dads, home-engineer moms, high school students, graduate students, brilliant professors, presidents, and heads of state.

When I care for every human being as a special creation of God, in His own image (Genesis 1:26–27), I realize that I have no right to underestimate a person's abilities. If that person is not functioning as I expect, the problem may not be with that individual. It could be the wrong job or a lack of recognition of their personal talents, traits, and intrinsic motivators.

I was able to take uneducated workers and help them become skilled jig-boring machine operators. I was able to take tough-acting, alcoholic workers from the third shift and help them become the most diligent and efficient workers they could become. I was able to take failing students and make them some of the best ones ever. I did this because I cared for each of them genuinely. I said to myself, "Lord, who am I to insult Your intelligence when it comes to Your specially created human beings? You care for even a sparrow, let alone a precious human being." When we care for people, they're eager to help themselves, and they are inspired to help you. What else can you ask for?

Step 2: Expectation

After creating a caring environment, the second important step in motivating someone is to specify the expectation and make sure the person clearly understands the expectations. When I analyze any situation with a lack of motivation, I almost always find that the expectation has not been specified at all or not clearly enough. So many misunderstandings come when this step is not being recognized and followed.

Problems and expectations are related directly. A problem occurs when an undesirable or unhappy situation occurs because experience is below expectation, and it is significantly perceived (figure 6.2)

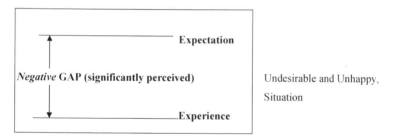

Fig 6.2 An **Undesirable and Unhappy Situation (Problem!)** occurs when Experience is below the Expectation, and is Significantly so Perceived.

When the gap between experience and expectation is positive—and perceived as such—it is a desirable, happy, or even delightful situation (see figure 6.3).

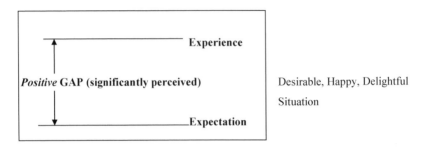

Fig 6.3 A **Desirable, Happy, and/or Delightful Situation** occurs when Experience exceeds Expectation Significantly, and is so Perceived.

I see a consistently delightful scenario when I apply this thinking at home, in professional situations, or in my classrooms.

Example 1

After assigning the final project in my classes, I spell out all my detailed expectations for the project—purpose, scope, and objectives—and the format of the written report and verbal presentations. I then jokingly say to the students: "Ladies and Gentlemen, please see some of the samples of reports already done by your predecessors. They are excellent, but I know you're so competitive that you'd want to better the best. I am not asking you to give me a report of the caliber of a Lamborghini, but an Aston Martin will do. Please ask me questions if my expectations are unclear."

My students usually laugh at my statement, but I have raised the bar of expectation in their minds to give me better reports than previous students. I have challenged them to strive for superb quality. My students always exceed my expectations and create a positive gap (figure 6.3). They are delighted by their performance, and I am delighted by their performance.

The opposite used to be true when I said, "Ladies and Gentlemen, here are the purpose, scope, and objectives for the report. Use your creativity and do the best report and presentation possible." There used to be a wide variation in the quality of reports and presentations, and we were all somewhat disappointed by the negative gap (figure 6.2).

Example 2

When our boys were teenagers, I used to work in the yard, wash our cars, and do other chores during weekends and summer breaks. One weekend, my wife wanted me to plant a rose garden. I measured out the area and told my sons, "Our purpose is to please your mom, and our objective is to remove the grass. The football game begins at four o'clock. We're going to do this as a team; we can take short breaks, but the job must be done if we want to watch the game from the beginning."

Johnny, our eldest son, diligently dug with me—with very few breaks. Paul, our youngest, would bring us water or soft drinks and entertain us with corny jokes and hilarious imitations. Because my expectations were clearly specified to both our sons as to the purpose (to please Mom) and the reward (to watch the football game without missing any part of it) while recognizing their differing intrinsic motivations, the job got done. We watched the game from the beginning as a satisfied bunch, and my wife was delighted at the prospect of planting her garden. The gap between expectation and experience was positive (figure 6.3).

I could have said, "Sons, we need to make a garden for your mom. Let's just do it." That would have resulted in unclear expectations (no target time to complete, no specified area of the patch). I might have been thinking the job should be done by four o'clock, but the kids would have only completed half the work by that time, thinking they could do the remaining work the next day or the next weekend. I would have grumbled and thought, *We would have enjoyed the game, but not with a clear mind.* We would have had a dissatisfied "customer," namely my wife. If Mom isn't happy, no one else is. This negative gap (figure 6.2) was avoided with very clear expectations.

Step 3: Positive Reinforcement

The third important step in the CEP model of motivation is positive reinforcement (P). It's basically reinforcing the actions a person has taken in a manner that is positive to further enable that person to repeat the behavior.

When you were walking toward your parents for the first time, you were falling a bit but getting up and stepping toward them. They cheered you on and said, "Come along, child. You are doing so well. Come on. You can do it." Unfortunately, in many families, positive reinforcement disappears as the children become teenagers. All of a sudden, instead of positive reinforcement, there is negative reinforcement: "Why can't you act like your brother? You are always messing up. You never listen to me." Negative reinforcement stifles good behavior and leads to indifference, resentment, hatred, and rebellion.

Undoing the damage of negative reinforcement takes so much effort and time. Positive reinforcement gives encouragement and confidence and becomes a source of kindness, gentleness, understanding, patience, love, and a successful attitude.

In the CEP model, even if the first two steps—caring and expectation—are done correctly but the third step, positive reinforcement, is absent, there will not be good and sustainable motivation.

The interesting thing about positive reinforcement is that it takes little effort and time, and it costs so little. In fact, it can be done in a few seconds—or a couple of minutes at the most. "Son, the way you played at the piano recital was so heartwarming and outstanding. I could never have done that." That sincere statement of positive reinforcement would've taken just a few seconds, but it would've gone a long way to bolster my son's confidence for his next recital.

There are a few rules to remember while giving positive reinforcement:

1. Immediacy. Don't wait a day or a week to offer positive reinforcement. Do it as soon as the positive behavior occurs. Ever noticed how all the animal and bird trainers follow this rule?

2. Sincerity. Your praise must be sincere and not superficial or just for the sake of doing it. This is important to note. In my praise, I said, "I could never have done that." My son knew that was true because I never could play piano. When we praise our children, they'd normally say, "Well, Dad, thank you, but you're biased from being my dad." When my compliment is sincere, they really believe those words of encouragement.

3. Specificity. It's important that your praise is specific. In this recital, I characterized his performance as "heartwarming." In another joint recital, I said, "Son, you and your brother synchronized your parts so beautifully that the harmony of your rendition was evident."

4. No Buts. Never use "but" in statements of positive reinforcement because the effect of what you're trying to say is lost in the "but." The qualifier reduces the positive effect or even nullifies the positive reinforcement. For example, if I had said, "Son, you were just outstanding, *but* you seemed just a notch off in the beginning of your rendition," this would have taken away the positive effect of my compliment. It would have made him think, *My dad is never satisfied 100 percent—no matter what a great job I do.*

Our son, Johnny, applied the CEP model (without even him recognizing it) on our little doggy, Julie, many years ago. She was one happy puppy because he cared for her so much. He was the one who named her "Julie." He expected her to learn what he was going to teach and not pick up a Cheerio or a piece of meat until she was told to eat. He positively reinforced her when she obeyed him by saying, "Julie is a good dog." Since dogs remember at least forty commands, what he taught her when she was tiny worked all her life (fourteen years). Our visitors were surprised to see what a disciplined, lovely dog she was. All it took was the CEP approach.

I have been applying my CEP model of motivation for more than fifty years, and I have never had to fail a student. My students think I am a tough teacher, but they also know I am the most caring one. In my six years as a full-time process engineer, industrial engineer, and manager, I never had to reprimand, lay off, or fire an employee.

In the Bible, Barnabas was considered one of the most effective motivators and encouragers. He encouraged the newly called apostle Paul constantly—even when the latter faced perilous times (Acts 11:22–26; 12:25–13:3, 15:35). Sometimes, honest disagreements occur among well-wishers as with Barnabas and Paul (Acts 15:36–40), but in a caring, expectant, and positively reinforcing environment, there is a less of chance of ill feelings.

King Solomon, through God's wisdom, recognized that building confidence is one of the best ways to motivate people. God is ultimately the greatest motivator: "The Lord will be your confidence" (Proverbs 3:26). He taught me how to motivate others with His caring, expectant, and positive reinforcement—every day for the seventy-four years I've known Him.

To sum up this motivation model, remember C-E-P. Practice it regularly at home, in the workplace, in social and religious gatherings, and wherever else you come across people. You'll discover the marvelous sense of fulfillment that comes from motivating people. It doesn't take much to bring the best out of people.

Motivating Your Spouse

Have you ever wondered why it is so much easier to motivate people *outside* your family than *in* your family? Within a few years of marriage, why is there so much acrimony between husband and wife? A few years ago, they would say, "Darling, I cannot live without you even for a moment." Today, they're saying, "I just can't stand you.

We're so different. You *never* listen to me or do what *I* would like you to do."

How can spouses motivate each other? It's extremely hard—and sometimes even impossible—unless you understand the factors that affect God's wisdom. The CEP model is a proven tool for motivating your spouse. Let's analyze what's needed in each of its three steps to work effectively.

The husband is asked to love his wife "just as Christ also loved the church and gave Himself to her" (Ephesians 5:25). Husbands are asked to love their wives just as they would care for their own bodies (Ephesians 5:28). In fact, the apostle Paul says, "He who loves his wife loves himself" (Ephesians 5:28). Peter asks husbands to live with their wives—understanding them and honoring them so that their prayers are not hindered (1 Peter 3:7).

Thus, a husband will create a caring environment for his wife when he does three things:

1. loves her as he loves himself
2. shows understanding
3. honors her

Very few husbands, including myself, can say that we do these three things sufficiently. God's wisdom tells us to make our wives feel special—like the princesses they dreamed of during their teenage years. After nearly fifty years of marriage, I am still learning how to love my wife, as myself, be a husband of understanding, and honor her by putting her on a pedestal. God is always right. When I make a concerted effort to do all these three things, I notice the positive outcomes immediately, but when I lack in even one of the three, I create difficult situations that are hard to extricate myself from.

How should husbands establish positive expectations with their wives? Well, the same way God expects of them as husbands. Through the prophet Micah, God declares that He requires three things of us (Micah 6:8):

1. justice
2. mercy
3. humility

Thus, when a husband shows justice by being fair to his wife, she will naturally reciprocate it to her husband. I realized my unfairness when I would question a hundred times the few dollars she spent on something for our home, but I could go out and buy a $30,000 car one day.

Being merciful is not always easy, but "blessed are the merciful, for they shall obtain mercy" (Matthew 5:7). What is mercy? Mercy is that we deserve punishment, but we are spared from it. Being merciful is a noble human attribute, but it doesn't come to us naturally. Those who have experienced God's infinite mercy should extend that same mercy to others. In the husband-wife relationship, the expectation on both sides should be mercy—as God Himself shows us that every single day in our lives.

Positive Reinforcement

It is through positive reinforcement that God wants husbands to honor their wives by expressing that their wives occupy the most important place in their lives. Public honor is even better. When you praise your wife publicly, it is extremely powerful positive reinforcement. Psychologists tell us that one of the best ways to love your wife is to honor her in front of children and friends and in social gatherings.

As we mature in our marriages, spouses become companions and friends who honor each other in a natural way. No effort is needed to showcase our spouses in public gatherings. While they may feel a bit embarrassed, in their heart of hearts, they appreciate it.

To summarize this section, a husband who loves his wife as himself understands her, honors her, and can be very effective in being able to have his wife do things for him with eagerness, spontaneity, and joy.

Motivating Your Children (Especially Teenagers)

Those of us who've had teenage children know how challenging the adolescent period can be for the parents and the children. The experience seems particularly memorable with the first one because we make most of our mistakes on them.

Teenage years are one of the most difficult periods of adjustment—spiritually, emotionally, and physically. Adolescents are neither men nor women yet, but they want to act like adults. They are in that awkward physical stage where their hormones are changing. Girls are becoming young women, and boys are becoming young men. Peer pressure is intense and unending. Those four or five years seem like forever for the growing and the grown-ups. During such extraordinary changes, it is difficult to delegate tasks to teenage children and see them do them according to your expectations. However, the CEP model of motivation applies here as well. Let's consider the three steps again.

The caring part is an extremely important step when dealing with teenagers because they want to see many things in terms of their parents' behaviors toward them:

1. affirmation
2. empathy
3. enthusiasm
4. friendship
5. honesty
6. openness
7. tolerance
8. understanding

Interestingly, when teenagers first see such a caring environment, they respect and desire their parents' wisdom.

Teenagers want to feel loved, but from a distance—or so it seems. They love you as much as they love their friends, but they are exploring friendships and relationships with their peers. They are testing and validating those relationships. They're alternating between "inclusive" and "exclusive" models of behavior. Sometimes, they want certain friends in their emotional territory, and at other times, they simply want them out. Their "adjustments" can create a perception of indecisiveness and immaturity from their parents' standpoint, but part of the reason for this is the physiological transition. The ways they dress, walk, talk, and study seem so different from the way they were just a few years ago. Many parents begin to judge their children with different lenses. Misunderstandings quickly move from the minor *I'm-sorry* stage to the major *I-hate-you* stage.

Hopefully, all that we learned in the communication chapter will come in handy here. Expert Christian psychologists like Dr. James Dobson remind us that the young adolescent stage is a passing phase in a person's life and that things will return to "normal" by the time they're nineteen or twenty, which is when the hormonal transition has stabilized.

The key to creating a caring atmosphere for teenagers is to remember the eight things listed above and ensure they're present in all the situations for the teenagers.

From God's perspective, children have to obey and honor their parents. It's important for parents to remember that they are expected to act according to their parental roles, and they must draw the line when necessary without being afraid of their children. They have to care for their children and not assert their privileges all the time. If they do so only in exceptional situations, they will be respected even more. Anything done in excess is ineffective. My personal way of communicating with my two boys when they were teenagers was to give the rationale for my decisions instead of simply declaring, "Because I said so."

The second step—establishing expectations—is critical for motivating young men and women. What we expect of them must honor God, be clearly understood on both sides, and be significant.

King David's expectations of his sons—Amnon and Absalom— did not satisfy any of the above three criteria. The result? Amnon raped his half sister, Tamar, and Absalom took revenge on Amnon by murdering him in cold blood.

Teenagers respond amazingly to expectations that meet the above criteria. I applied this thinking when I had to motivate my boys in their teenage years—with effective results every time.

During the past fifty-plus years, I've been able to demonstrate that the CEP model of motivation works successfully on university students. On the first day of the semester, I tell them that I care for them just like my own children, that I'll do everything I can to help them succeed, and that they count on me as a friend (if they wish to). I spell out my expectations as follows:

1. I want to set you up for success in this course and not for failure. None of you could fail this course, even if you tried because, as a professor, I'll make the course as interesting as possible. You'll do things in this course because you want to and not because you have to.
2. Here's the course outline. We'll go through this in detail and make sure you clearly understand my expectations.
3. You should never be afraid to ask questions. I don't mind explaining until you feel completely satisfied. No question is too unintelligent to be asked.
4. The homework requirements are spelled out in detail. You can work on these jointly, but I will ask you, at random, to come up to the board, solve the problem, and explain it to the class.
5. For everything done beyond my expectations, you earn bonus points (BPs), and these BPs are basically grade points. You can move up by as much as one grade by earning these bonus points. I give them examples of the way the BPs could change their grade from B+ to A– or A– to A. The maximum number of BPs earned the last time I taught this course was such and such. I know you want to beat that record, don't you?

6. I will assign only one A+ in this class. Even though, in terms of grades, both A and A+ amount to 4.0, it's a matter of prestige.

7. Attendance is not a requirement in my class, but I have seen, over the years, that if you miss even one lecture, it'll take so much effort to catch up and not fall behind. During all my years of teaching, only one student earned an A–without attending all my lectures. When you must miss a lecture, please let me know ahead of time.

8. If you're in a group project and will be out of town or are unable to attend class, you must still do your part for the team.

9. The bottom line is this: You have so much potential, and I want to help you realize it for yourself.

10. We're a team. Together, we'll make it happen. Excellence should be our starting point, and perfection is our ultimate goal. If you work hard, expecting no less than the best, you will achieve your best.

11. You're not merely a number in this class. I'll get to know you by name, and I will never forget you. So, let's get to work.

With this kind of an approach, and constantly encouraging them, it's been a wonderful experience for the students and for me. They succeed beyond their expectations, and I am a small part of their success.

The third part of the CEP model is positive reinforcement. With teenagers, as with any age, positive reinforcement is the essential step. Progress is made toward achieving expectations.

Positive reinforcement for teenagers can take several forms:

1. Literally "patting on the back" (when allowed) and saying, "I'm so proud of you."

2. "You've achieved quite a bit toward the expectations. I know you're capable of succeeding in your efforts."

3. "You may be discouraged that things aren't moving as you expected, but I think you're on the right track. If you need help, I'm here. Don't hesitate. By the way, did you think of this?"

4. If you know the teenager very well, like a family member, relative, or close family friend, you can give more of personalized comments—without violating university protocols—and recognize their efforts.

Teenagers need affirmations more than we think they do. You can never "over-affirm" a teenager. That stays with them for many years. Some of my former students, forty-five years or more after taking my courses, have told me about a specific affirmation they've carried in their hearts and how much it meant to them.

To summarize this chapter, a family unit and its members are always in need of motivating someone inside or outside the family. While there are many approaches to motivation, the three-step CEP model is always effective. This approach works in important and common situations. As with any tool or technique, practice makes it perfect. I have used it successfully for more than fifty years. If I can do it, you can too. The wisdom for this approach is derived from God's love, which is unconditional and freely available to every human being.

Three Actions I Can Take for One Month after Reading This Chapter

1.
2.
3.

Chapter Seven
DELEGATING

And when He had called His twelve disciples to Him, He gave them power over unclean spirits, to cast them out, and to heal all kinds of sickness and all kinds of disease.
—MATTHEW 10:1

Delegation is a very important managerial function in corporations and in families. However, there are many concepts about delegating that we don't seem to know about. We might misperceive, misapply, or forego the wonderful joy of seeing it used as a "people-building" function.

The Five Misconceptions about Delegation

Over the years, while observing people in more than one hundred countries, I have noticed some common misconceptions about delegation in all these countries.

Evading Responsibility

Many think that people delegate because they want to avoid work or responsibility. Delegation is often misunderstood as passing the buck. If the primary intent of delegation is avoiding work or responsibility, it's not delegation.

Avoiding Blame

Sometimes, small committees are formed to come up with recommendations that may be controversial or devastating for individuals, groups, or organizations. Individuals who do not want to be the bad guys may be perceived as having set up the committee to keep themselves safe from the wrath of the affected. This can be true sometimes, but it is not always the case. If the intent is to make someone a scapegoat, then it's not delegation.

Keeping People Busy

Some bosses delegate work to their employees just to keep them busy—even if their activities contribute very little to the objectives and goals of the organization. This happens more frequently when a boss goes on a long business trip or a vacation. Well, if the intent of delegation is about activities rather than objectives, then it's not delegation. This can happen in families too.

Demoting

Some organizations use delegation as a dirty trick for demoting someone from a position of power or influence. They delegate an unreasonable amount of responsibility and workload to someone who cannot handle it. When the aim is getting rid of someone, that's not delegation. The same thing can happen in families.

Being Mean

In some organizations and family units, meanness and a vengeful spirit are the motives for delegating excessive levels of work to someone they don't like. In the famous fable of Cinderella, the ill treatment from her stepmother offers a visual image of this kind of delegation. If the intent is to treat someone with disdain or to try to get revenge, it's not delegation, especially in a family.

What Is Delegation?

Delegation is seeking the help of one or more persons to accomplish an objective by assigning tasks, jobs, or projects and to bring out the best in people by identifying their unique talents, skills, and core competencies. Delegation can be a powerful, positive, and "people-building" tool in family units, corporations, and governments. Delegation has two fundamental aspects: to seek help to accomplish an objective and to bring the best out of those who have helped.

Accomplishing an objective might involve projects, jobs, or tasks. Tasks make up a job, and jobs make up a project. For example, grinding the condiments into a spicy paste is a task; cooking a chicken curry with this paste is a job; and hosting a dinner with the chicken curry as a dish is a project.

An excellent delegator—a mother with a daughter, son, and husband—might have noticed that her son likes gadgets and delegates him the task of grinding the condiments in a grinder. Her daughter, who enjoys experimenting with different types of cuisine, gets delegated the responsibility of preparing the chicken curry. She delegates her husband the task of setting the table since he has an artistic eye. As the hostess (project manager) for the dinner, she manages all of these tasks to bring joy to her guests.

Consider a supervisor who delegates various tasks and jobs to his employees in such a way that he brings out the best in them professionally and personally. All the projects he undertakes are done effectively and efficiently—and with great fun and enthusiasm. This supervisor recognizes both aspects of delegation: seeking help to accomplish his objectives and with a people-building intent (and not an exploitative intent)

True delegation must satisfy four conditions:

1. Delegation is seeking help by nature. Therefore, helpers are cared for and not used or exploited.
2. Personal and group accountability is not compromised with respect to the expected results.
3. Responsibility is assigned, but accountability is exacted.
4. There must be excitement and fun in doing tasks, jobs, and projects—with a celebration at the end.

The Six Reasons Why We Hesitate to Delegate

Why do so many people find it hard to delegate? Family members, especially moms, can get weighed down, dejected, and overwhelmed with work if they don't delegate. There are many reasons for not delegating and not lessening the daily pressures of life:

Superiority Complex

Many people think that no one else can do the job better than they can. After all, they have been doing it for so long with such affirmations and accolades that they doubt whether someone with a fraction of their experience could do the job as wonderfully as they've been able to. They forget that someone taught them to do the tasks or at least gave a chance to do them at one time. They think they are superior to others.

Inferiority Complex

What if I delegate this important task to another—and they execute it better than I did? Perhaps someone who appreciated me thus far might take away my future opportunities? These kinds of questions cross a person's mind, especially if they feel inferior to others. This mindset can prevent someone from delegating work to others.

Perception of Being Uncaring

Many people delegate work to others to reduce their workloads. They think it's not their business to be caring and considerate about it. They think they have the authority to assign the work, and they expect it to be done—irrespective of their personal fit for the tasks, their intrinsic and extrinsic motivation levels (see the chapter on motivation), and their professional goals. So many people don't delegate work to others lest they be perceived as uncaring, especially in churches and religious institutions as with parents who are the choleric type (for more information on the personality types, read Tim LaHaye's *I Love You, but Why Are We So Different?*).

Fear of Delegating to the More Experienced

When someone younger or less experienced must delegate work to a more experienced or older person, there is a certain level of intimidation. This can be stronger in cultures where age and experience are symbols of respect.

Lack of Competence

I have seen managers with nontechnical backgrounds hesitate to delegate work to technical personnel because they lack technical competence in the field. Even within technical ranks, some people are hesitant to delegate because they lack the expertise in that area. The same mindset can be true in families.

Past Experiences of Delegation

Some people don't want to delegate because their previous experiences were not positive. They don't want to waste their time and energy on more negative performances. If this happens in a family, resentments can be the result. Moses was overburdened while dealing with other people's problems during their forty-year wilderness journey. Fortunately, his father-in-law, Jethro, observed him carefully and suggested delegating so that Moses would hear only the most critical issues.

The Cardinal Mistake in Delegating

If we closely examine the reasons for hesitating to delegate, we see that the fundamental factor common to all of them is a lack of understanding of the second objective of delegation: "people-building." In other words, the two managerial functions—delegation and motivation—are interrelated. When our objective in delegation is only to accomplish a task, job, or project, it may or may not lead to positive motivation. However, when we correctly realize the dual intent of delegation (figure 7.1)—goal accomplishment and people-building—we achieve our goals and motivate those who are helping us.

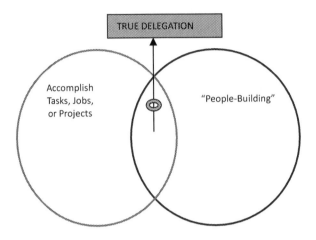

Fig. 7.1 The Dual Intents of Delegation

The flip side of ignoring the positive motivation part of the delegation function is tantamount to selfishness. Selfishness is the cardinal mistake of delegation because once people perceive that their interests are not important to the delegator, they only do the job because they must and not because they want to. If delegation is a win-lose proposition with the delegator, then that delegation is not a true delegation according to my definition. True delegation is a win-win for the delegator and the delegated.

The first incident of true delegation occurred when God brought all the animals and birds to Adam and empowered him to name them (Genesis 2:19–20). God could have given the names to the animals and birds that He created, but He chose to build up Adam's stature as the first human being and give him a sense of ownership of the stewardship function he would assume.

Nehemiah was a wall rebuilder and a people-builder when he delegated the responsibility of rebuilding the wall of Jerusalem in 446 BC (Nehemiah 3). Nearly two thousand years ago, Jesus commanded His disciples to go and preach the good news all over the world. He reinforced His confidence in them by declaring that He was passing on His authority from the heavenly Father to them to preach the Gospel (Matthew 28:18–20).

Jesus never asked His disciples to do anything that He Himself did not do first (except being crucified for redemption of humanity's sins.) He was never selfish. He was a true delegator and a people-builder in the purest sense of the terms. Is it any wonder then, even two thousand years later, that the good news is reaching millions of people around the world?

Conventional versus MDF Formula for Delegation

Many people correctly assign the responsibilities and authority and spell out the accountability expected, but the work doesn't get done the way it was expected—on or before the target date and at or below the target cost. Why? Because they are delegating via conventional wisdom (figure 7.2).

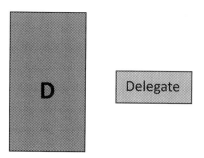

Fig 7.2 Traditional Approach to Delegation (Sporadic Results)

Two other steps are necessary to make delegation productive. The person being delegated (the delegate) must be motivated. They must know why the work is being assigned to them and not to someone else. Even if motivation precedes delegation, the job may not get done according to expectations. To ensure that it does, the person delegating the work (the delegator) must follow up. Otherwise, no matter how well the delegator motivated the delegate and clearly assigned the responsibilities with appropriate authority, the job may not get done as expected. The formula for delegating for best results is M (motivate), D (delegate), and F (follow up) (figure 7.3).

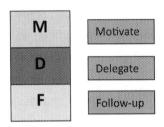

Fig 7.3 Sumanth's *"MDF Formula"* for Delegation (for Consistently Excellent Results)

Scenario 1: A Traditional Approach to Delegating (See Figure 7.2)

Jack, the boss, calls one of his employees, Bryan, and says, "We have this project for one of our biggest clients. It needs to be completed by Friday. I want you to take care of this segment of the project, and I want a progress report by Friday at four o'clock."

Bryan works the whole week—even staying late every day—while his new wife, Jill, has been waiting and hoping he'd take her out for a movie and a nice dinner. Bryan says, "Honey, I'm so sorry, but this project has come at a bad time for us. I promise I'll make up for this after I turn in the progress report to Jack on Friday."

Bryan completes his part of the project by 3:55 on Friday afternoon, and rushes to Jack's office, wanting to thrill his boss.

Jack's secretary says, "He's on a family vacation for two weeks in Colorado Springs."

"Did Jack leave a message for me to turn in the report he said he urgently needed?"

"No," replies his secretary.

Two weeks later, Jack calls Bryan to his office.

Bryan can't wait to show his report.

Jack says, "Bryan, I have this new project for one of our most important clients. We're late on this. I would like you to work on it and give me a report on Wednesday."

"Sir, what about this report you wanted two weeks ago? I worked on it day and night."

"Oh, that report? We don't need it now, but this other project is really urgent."

On Wednesday, Jack waits for Bryan's report. By Thursday morning, Jack is fuming and fretting. "Bryan, I told you how important this project was. I was expecting to have your report yesterday evening before you went home."

"Oh, that project? sir, I didn't know it was that urgent. I haven't started working on it yet."

"What? You haven't even started?" Jack throws a temper tantrum.

When we analyze this scenario, what do we see? Jack lost credibility with the first project's misstated urgency, and Bryan didn't pay much attention to the second project. This was a classic case of delegation because of Jack's positional authority, and when he didn't motivate or follow up on the project report, the result demoralized Bryan—and he will probably never pay much attention to Jack's words. If a son is working in a family business, and Bryan and his dad, Jack, imagine the tense atmosphere at the dinner table that night.

Scenario 2: Sumanth's Approach to Delegating (See Figure 7.3)

On Monday morning, Jack calls in Bryan, sits him down, and says, "Bryan, we have this project for one of our biggest clients. It needs to be completed by Friday. I thought quite a bit about who to delegate this important segment of the project, which requires quite a few analytical steps and details. We can't afford to make any mistakes because of the nature of the project. For two years, I've been watching you carefully. You have consistently helped me with your excellent analytical capabilities and have a proven record of paying attention to details. You were the first person I thought of. Bryan, I know you're just married, and it's a bit unfair on my part to assign you this project with such a short deadline, but could you please help me out?"

"Sir, you're right. My wife and I were planning to spend at least a couple of nights out this week, but I understand the sense of urgency and the confidence you have in my abilities. I'll do my best."

"Thank you, Bryan. Do you think you can give me the report by four o'clock on Friday?"

"Yes, sir. I'll do whatever it takes to get it to you on Friday—no later than four thirty."

"That would be great. I'd appreciate that, Bryan. Thank you."

Bryan convinces Jill and works day and night, and he knocks on Jack's door at four o'clock on Friday.

Jack's secretary says, "He's left on an unexpected two-week family time, but he wanted me to overnight your report to him. Before I go home this evening, Jack wants me to take your home phone number. He will contact you this weekend if he needs any clarifications on your report."

On Saturday morning, Jack calls Bryan and says "I'm sorry I couldn't be there yesterday to receive your report in person. I had an unexpected family situation to take care of. Thank you so much for sending me your report. I've gone through it. It looks like another winner. You've really outdone yourself. Thank you so much for your diligence and for going beyond the call of duty. Please apologize to your wife on my behalf."

"No problem, sir. I appreciate your confidence. I hope your family situation is under control."

"Bryan, I want you take off Monday and make up for the lost time with your wife. Make it a long weekend."

Bryan is overjoyed.

Two weeks later, when Jack assigns the next urgent project to Bryan, do you think he'll meet the deadline? Of course! Bryan knows his boss assigns him projects because of his confidence in his abilities. Jack sincerely appreciates his work, doesn't lie about the sense of urgency, and follows up on target dates. Jack genuinely cares about Bryan's family responsibilities.

In this scenario, Jack applied the MDF formula of delegation:

1. motivating Bryan before delegating the project
2. delegating the project with specificity and a clear deadline
3. following up on the assignment after delegating

Jack also gave an unexpected reward to Bryan (taking off Monday). The MDF formula will always give better results than traditional approaches to delegating. Throwing in a surprise reward for a diligent effort is icing on the cake.

As a father, I applied the MDF formula many times with my sons and had fantastic results—even when they were teenagers. Families will accomplish so much more—in everything from taking out the garbage to going on an international family vacation—when every member applies the MDF formula when delegating.

Reverse Delegation: The Ultimate Art

It's quite natural for a boss to delegate work to an assistant, a father to a child, or an older sibling to a younger one. What about the assistant delegating work to the boss? When the latter happens, I call it *reverse delegation.*

Reverse delegation is delegating work from the usual *delegate* to the *delegator.* When you take the art of delegation to the point of reverse delegation, you've mastered it. During the last fifty-plus years, I got things done by my superiors, including professors when I was a student, my boss when I was his assistant, my sister, and my senior colleagues at the university. Some points must be remembered while doing reverse delegation:

1. Don't overdo it. Reverse delegation, if practiced on a regular basis, indicates a defective behavior, and it shows that you

don't respect your superior's position and time. You may be exploiting your bosses rather than leveraging their influence for the common good.

2. Don't do it if you haven't mastered the MDF formula. We have seen how poor the results will be with the traditional concept of delegation (figure 7.2) and how much better the outcome would be if the MDF formula was applied (figure 7.3). It takes years to become good at this. If you try to use reverse delegation without knowing the art of MDF, you could fall flat on your face and embarrass yourself by being snubbed or ridiculed.

3. Don't use it insensitively. You must understand the cultural context when you do reverse delegation. In many Eastern cultures, reverse delegation is considered impolite and insulting. If a personal assistant delegates a job to the chief minister in India, the former could lose their job in no time.

Reverse delegation is only for experienced delegators. It can work relatively easily in the home settings since parents don't mind doing things for their children, but that is not the case in work settings where the boss does not expect to do their assistant's work unless it is an extenuating circumstance.

We conclude this chapter by pointing out the following important truths:

1. Delegation is a highly misunderstood concept.
2. The concept of true delegation involves getting work done and building up people.
3. The MDF formula for delegation gives consistently excellent results.
4. The ultimate mastery of delegating is when one can do reverse delegation.
5. When true delegation concepts are applied, you'll be able to seek help from people to get things done, enlarge your sphere

of positive influence, and become another important agent of God's goodness and love.

Three Actions I Can Take for One Month after Reading This Chapter

1.
2.
3.

Chapter Eight

FINANCIAL CONTROL IN THE FAMILY

The wicked borrows and does not repay, but the righteous shows mercy and gives.
—PSALM 37:21

The moment we mention the word *money*, many images pop up in our minds. Some people associate money with making a living, security, prestige, self-reliance, or self-sufficiency. Others relate money to materialism, selfishness, corruption, false prestige, evil, strained relationships, greed, covetousness, or arrogance. Depending upon the situation, every one of these characterizations may be accurate, though not necessarily right, for the goodness and well-being of people. Well, what about money in the context of family management?

The Seven Reasons for Money as a Critical Source for Family Conflicts

One of the biggest issues in marriages is money, and there are some common reasons for this:

Lack of Contentment

No matter how much money is earned by a family unit, lack of contentment forces the family to earn more, which strains many other aspects of life. Covetousness and greed are at the heart of this behavior. Comparisons of money and status with neighbors, friends, and colleagues causes the mindset of no contentment. As humans, it's quite natural for us to imitate others. Therefore, we can easily fall into a money trap if we are not careful. The Bible reminds us: "Let your conduct be without covetousness; be content with such things as you have. For He Himself has said, 'I will never leave you nor forsake you'" (Hebrews 13:5).

Lack of Self-Discipline in Using Money

Many families don't have a proper, disciplined approach to managing money. If you run your family finances on a budget, you may be an exception. While I was growing up, and even until I was in my thirties, managing money was a simple concept. I could spend only if I had cash in my hand. In the name of technological sophistication, our lives have been subjected to unneeded complexity, including credit cards, home equity loans, signature loans, 100 percent financing, and reverse mortgages. Technology has reached a point where it is controlling us—we are not controlling it. Under the guise of convenience, we fall into financial traps that some people never recover from. There are people—ironically, mostly the poor—who are paying twice or even three times the interest rate of a self-disciplined money caretaker—for everything from cars to dishwashers. While a bank's interest income from loans to such individuals surges, the poor person's principal amount on loans remains mostly unchanged. Some have come to a state of repaying one loan with another.

Lack of Proper Perspective on Money

In a consumerism-oriented world like ours, we are conditioned by the wrong messages on TV, social media, radio, internet, smartphones, and digital assistants. They preach about the false and irrelevant need of having things and the false notion that money will bring lasting happiness, prestige, status, fame, self-sufficiency, and financial freedom. A financial planner told me forty years ago that he'd be financially free within five years, but he's still working full-time to make ends meet. Howard Hughes, the founder of Hughes Aircraft, was one of the richest men of his time, yet few would say he lived a happy life, especially during his last days. Those who think money is an end by itself—rather than a tool—and go after it passionately often end up living miserably. Paul instructed Timothy, his protégé, and young pastor: "Command those who are rich in this present age not to be haughty, nor to trust in uncertain riches but in the living God, who gives us richly all things to enjoy" (1 Timothy 6:17).

Lack of a Secure Feeling

Some people who come from utter poverty resolve themselves to never go back to poverty. They try to amass as much wealth as possible. They don't let go of it. They save millions, but they don't give generously of their wealth, and when they die, their estates sometimes go uncollected. They live paranoid lives because they're afraid of losing financial security. While riches seem fleeting and temporal, followers of Christ have a financial anchor in Him. He is unchanging and reliable: "Jesus Christ is the same yesterday, today, and forever" (Hebrews 13:8). Being anchored in Him bring secure feelings to all areas of life.

Differing Priorities of Spouses

When husbands and wife have very differing priorities or concepts of money, they can expect problems with financial management. Until about fifteen years ago, one of my wrong priorities was replacing one of our cars every other year. I would buy a used car for $20,000 and somehow convince my wife it was a good decision. When she wanted to spend $1,000 on replacing an old piece of furniture, I'd fuss about that. Fairness? No, certainly not. When I recognized the problem, I was able to change. After all, Chaya was—and is—right. A car is just a means to take you from point A to point B. When it is reliable and looks reasonably nice, it should serve your purpose. She drives about five thousand miles a year while the national average is twelve thousand. I learned that my spending priorities must be reoriented. The money we save on cars goes to help in more worthy and life-fulfilling causes that affect poor and orphaned children. I, as the husband, can be fair by enabling Chaya to spend according to her discretion. I must trust in her wisdom, which is high.

Feeding Destructive Habits

Money spent on addictive habits can evaporate quickly. Alcoholism, betting, gambling, pornography, and other addictions can eat up money faster than it's available. The family's finances can be strained, and these habits can cause dangerous spiritual, emotional, and relational effects. They can destroy individuals and families—sometimes for generations to come. It's not worth it. Some husbands abuse their wives physically or emotionally after intoxication or during their wives' protests about this behavior. Destructive habits ruin families. It's easy to fall into the snares of so-called friends who convince us that everyone is doing it—or it's even lawful. The wise apostle Paul reminds us: "All things are lawful for me, but all things are not helpful" (1 Corinthians 6:12).

A Controlling Attitude

Money can become a control issue for a husband or wife. This is generally true with the sole breadwinning husband or wife. When the husband is the only one bringing home a paycheck and asks his wife for an account of every penny spent by her, it's a natural reaction to say, "Because I'm not working outside the home, you're humiliating me. I'm also going out to work." The wife here perceives a controlling attitude. Even if the perception is incorrect sometimes, if the husband feeds this perception continuously, it'll create many conversational sparks. The husband must be careful about how he explains his position to his wife—even when there is merit to his assertion. "Whoever loves money never has enough; whoever loves wealth is never satisfied with their income. This too is meaningless" (Ecclesiastes 5:10 NIV).

Correct Attitude toward Money

In His teachings, Jesus spent more time on money than on any other matter. Clearly, there must have been a reason for this. He knew that the way money was handled by a person said much about the spiritual well-being of that person. When we distill His perspectives on money, they boil down to five things:

1. We're simply the stewards of money. We don't own it. God does.
2. Money is simply a tool to accomplish an objective that adds value to humanity.
3. No one carries money with them when they die. How it is used after their death determines their priorities before their death.
4. Money is not evil by itself. The love of money is the root of all evil.

5. Those who are given the privilege of having much money have a greater responsibility to use it for good causes than those who are not.

The Ten Principles of Financial Control

Based on the wisdom from God's Word, we can practice sound money management and financial control by observing the following ten principles.

God First Principle

"Give God first His money." The tithe is one-tenth of all that God blesses us with. It represents one-tenth of the gross amount of a paycheck or one-tenth of the net income earned by family members or any other income that is honorable in God's sight. My mother taught us seventy-four years ago that one-tenth of our pocket money belongs to God. When we started getting paychecks, one-tenth of every paycheck belonged to God as a tithe—and the entire first paycheck.

My first paycheck was my graduate stipend of 150 rupees in 1967 (in those days, it was equivalent to twenty US dollars). Since it was my first paycheck, I gave it all to God. All my life, I have followed this principle every single month, and I can say confidently that there has never been a month when I could not fulfill all my family's financial obligations. This principle works 100 percent of the time— with the right attitude toward God's provision for our lives.

When God gave me a job, He gave me the health to do this job and other blessings associated with the use of His provision for me and my family. Without His protective eye, in one short instant, I could have lost the opportunity to do my job. Yet, by offering him the tithe (10 percent), I was keeping 90 percent of my income. He only asks for 10 percent. However, it's the first 10 percent that must be offered to Him before we use the other 90 percent He has blessed us with.

The attitude we take while offering the first one-tenth to God is important. The first check I write before I write any other check for anything else is always the tithe check to my church, which is the "storehouse." God does not really need our money. He created and owns everything in this world. He is really observing our attitude toward His provision and blessing to us. Before the days of direct deposit, my wife and I would hold the paycheck in our hands, pray, and thank God for His provision. I'd write the first check for the tithe to our church, and then I'd cash it at the bank for some spending money.

God loves a cheerful giver:

> He who sows sparingly will also reap sparingly, and he who sows bountifully will also reap bountifully. So let each one give as he purposes in his heart and not grudgingly or of necessity; for God loves a cheerful giver. And God is able to make all grace abound toward you, that you, always having all sufficiency in all things, may have an abundance for every good work. (2 Corinthians 9:6–8)

I write that first tithe check for my church with a grateful and joyful heart. I always have some money left at the end of the month—even when I have unexpected expenses. Having experienced this for fifty-four years, I know this is not a coincidence. It is God's unfailing promise kept. God never promises anything that He does not keep. That's a 100 percent guarantee.

When we don't have faith in His promise, we may rationalize by saying, "This month, I'll give Him from my net pay because I have this unexpected bill on my desk. I'm sure God will understand." Yes, God certainly understands, but the problem is a lack of faith in His promise. When we hold back what is His, we are robbing Him. It's that serious. Robbing God? Yes, "in tithes and offerings" (Malachi 3:8–10).

The few times I didn't trust God's promise, I'd incur unexpected expenses—car breaking down, an unexpected plumbing job, or a big bill. On the other hand, when I gave my tithe cheerfully, my electricity and phone bills were much lower than budgeted—or I had other cost avoidances, such as no car or plumbing issues.

I am not saying that we will always avoid unexpected expenses because we're faithful to God in our tithing. I am saying that He is always trustworthy—and He keeps His promises.

Nowhere in the Bible does God ask us to test Him except in the matter of tithing. He challenges us to test His faithfulness when we give Him our tithe (Malachi 3:10). If you've never tried giving your tithe cheerfully, try it for three months and see what you find:

> Honor the Lord with your possessions, and with the firstfruits of all your increases, so your barns will be filled with plenty, and your vats will overflow with new wine. (Proverbs 3:9–10)

When I am a diligent steward of God's money entrusted to me, I can picture Him taking care of my needs even before I express my intentions to Him.

The Faith Principle

"Trust God that He will supply all your needs all the time." This principle is from the wonderful declaration the apostle Paul made almost two thousand years ago:

> And my God shall supply all your needs according to His riches in glory by Christ Jesus. (Philippians 4:19)

It's a matter of trusting God for all our needs and not just some of them. God is loving, caring, and merciful. He disciplines us when we are disobedient to Him, but He is not angry forever. True trust in God comes when we can't see what He can do. In fact, that's why "faith is the substance of things hoped for, the evidence of things not seen" (Hebrews 11:1). Faith in God is evident when we trust Him despite our circumstances and irrespective of our seemingly desperate situations—whatever they may be.

Jesus teaches us that not even a sparrow falls to the ground without the Father's will. We should not be worried about our future since we're of more value than sparrows. One of the easiest images we can think of when entrusting our needs to God is to view Him as we do our earthly dads, especially when we were little kids. Remember those days? "Daddy, I got a boo-boo on my foot!" We would run to him, crying, and he would stretch out his arms and say, "It's okay, my son. Daddy will take care of it. Don't cry." God demonstrates the same kind of assuring faithfulness in our lives when we place our faith in Him.

He has never disappointed me when He promised me—not even once. Sometimes, He comes through on His promise at the last second, making us wait in desperate nervousness, but He knows what He's doing. When He shows up to meet our needs in the nick of time, He demonstrates that He's always trustworthy and faithful to His children. When we see our prayers answered this way, we tend to give all credit to Him; otherwise, we tend to assume that we had everything to do with it. "Without faith, it is impossible to please Him" (Hebrews 11:6).

The Needs/Wants Principle

"Keep your needs and wants in line with God's will." There's a big difference between wants and needs. Many of our wants and wish lists are self-indulging, self-gratifying, selfish, greedy, or covetous. Why should we blame God if we ask Him for things that He knows can harm us? For example, if I say, "Please, Lord, grant me enough money to buy that house," but if my income is unable to support the mortgage payment, is that something God should grant me? Of course not. I should be grateful that He didn't answer my immature prayer, sparing my family financial and emotional stress.

God answers our prayers in basically three ways: *yes, no,* or *not now.* When a family asks God for more income but wastes it on destructive habits such as gambling or alcoholism, and God says no—they should thank Him for preventing destruction of the family. When we want to ask Him to bless us with a large increase in salary when we haven't demonstrated our stewardship in our present salary, He is doing us a big favor by answering, "Not now."

Jesus intercedes for us with the heavenly Father, but the Bible says that He will ask the Father only according to His will. We shouldn't expect God to answer our prayers for financial needs—or any other needs—if they are not in line with God's will. Aren't we glad we have a great filtering system for our childish prayers? It sorts out requests in accordance with God's will from those that are not.

In short, God is always faithful when we put our money matters into His sovereign, all-knowing, all-powerful hands, and we have nothing to worry about. We must have the childlike faith to quit worrying about our finances—as long as we are following the first two principles of financial control.

Contentment is the best antidote to chase after wants. In fact, apostle Paul declares, "In whatever state I am to be content" (Philippians 4:11) and "Godliness with contentment is great gain" (1 Timothy 6:6).

The Cash/Credit Principle

This very important principle, considering the horrible levels of personal debt we're carrying, says the following: As much as possible and feasible, use cash or debit cards and not credit cards to manage your non-regular expenses. Corporate bankruptcies and personal bankruptcies in America are atrocious. This is clearly a symptom of our lack of discipline to control our expenses against our incomes.

Borrowing money is unwise: "The rich rules over the poor, and the borrower is servant to the lender" (Proverbs 22:7).

Sometimes old is gold. Even thirty years ago, most of us were using checks or cash for our transactions. We didn't write a check or dish out precious cash unless we had enough money in the bank to cover it. Today, due to credit cards, overdraft protections, margin loans on investments, electronic fund transfers, and automatic payments, we have virtually lost control over our take-home pay.

It seems as though we are good at creating problems unnecessarily, and then we try to solve them, often with suboptimal solutions. In the old days of cash-only transactions, we budgeted our expenses for most, if not all, of our non-regular expenses, such as books, dry cleaning, eating out, and gasoline, and we even used budget envelopes to manage our money. At the end of the month, we used to have some cash left in at least a few of those envelopes. What fun it was to see and feel this extra money.

Today, we cannot feel the cash or the luxury of having some money left in our bank accounts. For those having difficulty balancing their checkbooks, it is frustrating and stressful to see that the balance shown in the bank statement is much less than that in the checkbook, especially since the bank statements are not received until half the month is over. Adding fuel to the fire are overdraft fees or insufficient funds fees that eat away any savings.

On top of this, we are almost forced to keep track of our accounts on the computer. Having to learn about accounting terms like debits and credits and putting the wrong amounts in the wrong columns—and literally getting overwhelmed with electronic stress and anxiety—is not fun at all. What's all this for? We're like chickens running around without any sense of control. Is it any wonder that our lives are being wasted away, keeping pace with irrelevant tools and technologies instead of using our time for worthwhile causes? What happened to those good old days when we had simpler lives?

Old is gold in managing the non-regular expenses. The first month was a bit hard to get used to, but now it's routine. I have authorized AFT (automatic fund transfers) for all my regular expenses, such as tithes, groceries, electricity, telephone, water, internet, car insurance, and home insurance. After paying off our mortgage, I find it liberating to get out of what seemed like a never-ending financial black hole. I use just one credit card for gasoline, eating out, and travel. Another credit card is for expenses related to gifts for special occasions. I set the AFT payment for each credit card to be paid in full, which avoids any finance charges and builds an excellent credit score. Even while buying a car, I try to pay it off in one swoop. I use my checkbook for most of the payment, and if necessary, I charge a small amount to one of my unused credit cards, which gives me a chance to pay it off by the time I receive the next bank statement. I manage our other small expenses on a cash basis. This has been a wonderful thing for us.

Don't ask for unnecessary credit—and pay off your mortgage as soon as possible. We were able to pay off our thirty-year mortgage in twenty-two years by designating an extra payment every two weeks toward the principal. This saved us several thousands of dollars in interest. Don't use credit cards indiscriminately—people spend an average of 12 percent more than with cash—and select credit or cash option based on the concept of simplification, accountability, and tractability. Don't try to keep up with the Joneses. The blind leading the blind can be dangerous.

The Cost Avoidance Principle

"Avoid all possible costs in managing your money by preventing avoidable expenses and minimizing unavoidable expenses." The Bible instructs: "There is desirable treasure, and oil in the dwelling of the wise, but a foolish man squanders it" (Proverbs 21:20). So many household expenses are avoidable, but we don't take the necessary measures to prevent them from occurring:

1. Wear and tear on tires. Not inflating your tires regularly to the correct pressure or bumping into curbs or parking blocks can ruin the alignment, wear out the tires unevenly, and cost hundreds of dollars, especially with high-performance tires.

2. Going to grocery stores more than once a week. This wastes precious gasoline and precious time. It causes unnecessary emotional stress and arguments and deprives you of the little extra cash you'd have had at the end of the month—in addition to raising stress levels, which is bad for your health and family harmony.

3. Home maintenance and cleaning. If you ignore that biweekly weed pulling or monthly A/C filter cleaning, you'll find your landscaping maintenance costs rising dramatically and your AC annual maintenance bill will be several hundreds of dollars. If you don't weather-strip your home, you can easily spend several hundreds of dollars.

4. Carelessness. You're in a terrible hurry already and several minutes late for work, and you forget to press the garage door opener. Wham. You back into the garage door and have a hefty bill to pay despite your insurance coverage (unless you have a zero deductible). If you slam the car door a second before your young child releases his fingers from the doorpost, there will be a bad crying situation for both the child and you—plus half a day at the emergency room and a big hospital bill. All these preventable costs are due to carelessness and a lack of attention.

The Lending Principle

When you lend a large amount of money to friends or other people, it's best to have a written agreement—or at least get it notarized. Time and again, I have seen major misunderstandings popping up months or even years later. When the expectations of both parties are spelled out clearly in written form, opportunities for misunderstandings are eliminated or at least minimized.

In February 1970, my dad's closest friend's son wanted to rent my dad's home, which we vacated to move to our new home a few miles away. My father passed away in 1970 suddenly of a heart attack. Taking advantage of the situation, the son stopped sending his rent payments. When my mother wrote a letter asking him to vacate the house in view of his delinquent payment history, he refused. In my dad's papers, I located a legally executed agreement between my father and this troubling tenant. The latter was surprised that we had legal proof. Within a few months, with prayers and trusting God's justice—and the written legal agreement—he vacated the house on his own.

My mother and father taught my sister and me to always be generous and gracious to people but be businesslike when lending money. Following this principle can prevent lots of headaches and emotional stress—and legal expenses, especially if you lend large amounts of money. Even the best of friends and relatives can turn out to be your worst enemies when you're dealing with money matters.

The Banking Principle

"Whenever possible, do all your banking with one well-established, trustworthy, and reputed bank." Financial control ensures that you have a good handle on your money. This principle is quite relevant today. On March 10, 2023, Silicon Valley Bank shut down—and its funds were taken over by the US government. This was devastating to many tech companies.

In my thirties, I used to do my personal banking at two banks and my business banking at a third location. It got quite complex, and multiple bank statements were coming every month at different times. It was overwhelming to read the statements and reconcile my checkbooks at different times of the month. I was reading my bank statements more often than my favorite magazines. Thirty years later, it is much more stressful to manage three bank statements, three checkbooks, three sets of ATM transactions, and two mortgage accounts (a first mortgage and a home equity loan). If you add several credit card accounts, you have literally dozens of pages of statements to read and hundreds of transactions to post in your computer.

The electronic jungle today is as bad as the manual mess of thirty years ago. Several years ago, I started doing all my personal banking with just one institution. Even my home mortgage loan was through this one institution. This has saved me money and countless hours. This simplification, through consolidation, has been extremely productive for me. I look at my bank statements only once a month now.

The Investing Principle

"After investing at least 10 percent as tithing for God's work among the humanity, invest at least 10 percent of your gross income in a portfolio of savings, which, when used during your lifetime or after your passing, will benefit God's creation and God's children."

Jesus shared a parable about an owner who asked his three servants to invest the talents he gave them before going on a trip: five talents to the first servant, two to the second, and one to the third one. When the owner returned, he asked them how they had invested. He was happy with the first and the second servants since they doubled their investments. However, the owner was unhappy because the other buried his one talent without investing. The owner was furious with him for doing nothing with that one talent.

In complete obedience to God's love, we should first give our tithe, and every family unit must invest a portion of the income for the present and the future. The words in the investing principle have been chosen carefully. You should set aside at least 10 percent of your gross income after the tithe, but more is better. During the years of college education for children, maybe more is not feasible, but consistency is the key to proper investing. It's not just the amount that matters; it's the consistency. It is better to invest $100 each month ($1,200 a year) in a mutual fund than to invest $1,200 once a year in that same mutual fund. Financial experts can prove their veracity of this statement through the "dollar-averaging concept."

I let the savings I set aside every month be a part of an investment portfolio, which is basically a group of mutual funds. It may be best to consult with a professionally licensed financial advisor to help set this up. Teachers and professors have entities such as TIAA/CREF, which specialize in retirement portfolios for such individuals. There are many others. A professional financial advisor with integrity and experience can help set up an appropriate portfolio, considering your specific needs, goals, and risk tolerance.

Don't put all your eggs in one basket. This is the wisdom behind putting your savings in a portfolio rather than one type of savings. For example, instead of putting all my savings into regular savings accounts, certificates of deposits, mutual funds, individual stocks, and bonds, I let a financial advisor develop an investment portfolio that includes a little bit of all these and others that he knows of.

You should invest in savings for the benefit of your lifetime as well as your survivors, benefactors, and others who God created. He loves them all as His children. This is a loaded statement. Most people think of savings as money for a rainy day, but this is not a biblical approach.

Jesus clearly warned, "Where you treasure is, there your heart will be also" (Luke 12:34). He also said we should invest our treasures in heaven where there are no moths or rust to destroy. He was speaking in an allegorical sense. He was basically saying that we should invest in taking care of God's precious human beings in the present time and further His kingdom. His children shall inherit it after their physical death. He is advising us to think of our savings to benefit the poor, the fatherless, the widows, and the spiritual shepherds and servants who are advancing His Gospel.

Invest your time, talents, and treasures to honor and glorify God and to love and care for your fellow humans. Where and how we invest our God-given time, talents, and treasures is a great revealer of our priorities in life for now and for the future. Make your investments according to God's purposes for your life. He's the greatest financial advisor in the world, and you can never go wrong when you invest according to His advice.

The Balancing Principle

"Make a conscious effort to balance your financial stewardship responsibilities with your family's emotional needs and wants." This requires prioritizing our lives. Jesus advises the believers, "But seek first the kingdom of God and His righteousness, and all these things shall be added to you" (Matthew 6:33).

First and foremost, you must consciously or deliberately make a choice to balance your priorities. Your priorities are to please the One who created you, blesses you, and enables you to work and earn a living. He helps you save for the present and the future. You must love your fellow humans. When you balance these priorities, you'll experience inner joy and peace, which no money or wealth can ever offer. You are just a steward of what God has entrusted to you—and you are to provide for your family's needs and wants.

Recognizing the first reality means that we do not own anything. Everything belongs to God. He happens to entrust us for our lifetime the resources so that we can use them, add value to them, and return them ultimately to His care. This may sound radical, but here's the truth. Job was a righteous, wealthy man who had everything going for him. He had lots of wealth, good health, and a wonderful, happy family. When Satan challenged God to test Job with adversities and sufferings so that God's true allegiance to God would be revealed, God allowed Job to be subjected to a long and difficult period of sufferings.

Job's friends thought he was being punished, and they began to abandon him. Job's wife asked him to curse God and die, but Job's faithfulness to God was rock-solid. He never wavered. He said, "The Lord gave me, the Lord can take it away." His health, wealth, and children were taken away, yet he never got angry with God or showed his distrust in Him. He seems to have understood perfectly how to maintain his priorities: God first, family next, and everything else after that. What godly wisdom he had. In return for his absolute allegiance to God, his health, wealth, and children were restored to a much greater extent. The devil was defeated in his challenge—thanks to Job's dutifulness to God.

When we go through life's challenges, especially trials and tribulations, we may not always have such a happy ending as Job had. However, we can rest assured that God's grace is sufficient for us. God stays with us through our sufferings. He never abandons us. Nothing is allowed to happen to His children without His permission. He is sovereign. He is in perfect control of everything that happens to us. Why should we worry about anything at all? Maybe we can be concerned, but not worried, because we who have been adopted into His kingdom (by saving faith in His Son, Jesus Christ) have been assured that "all things work together for good to those who love God, to those who are called according to His purpose (Romans 8:28).

God will meet all our needs (Philippians 4:19) when we trust Him to do so. What about our wants? When God promised that He will give us the desires of our heart when we delight in Him, He keeps His promises, provided those desires are in line with His perfect will. For example, if you repeatedly ask God to have lots of wealth just like your neighbor—because of your covetousness—you shouldn't be surprised if His answer is no because your request goes against God's commandment that you shall not covet anything.

When we keep our spiritual, emotional, and financial priorities right in God's sight, we will be very grateful when God blesses us with things we never expected. We lead lives of contentment when He does not grant us the things we hoped for once in a while. His plans for us are always better than our plans for ourselves.

The Inheritance Principle

"Treat all your inheritance wealth with the same sense of stewardship for God as you would your own wealth." The Bible says, "A good man leaves an inheritance to his children's children" (Proverbs 13:22). What do their children do with that inheritance? I have met many people who inherited large amounts of wealth—property, cash, and valuable treasures—and squandered it quickly. I have discovered that there are two basic types of people who become rich inheritors: those who treat their inheritance with gratitude and responsible stewardship and those who squander it. How should an inheritance be thought of? This principle should help answer that question.

The inheritance wealth you may acquire could include cash, investment portfolios, tangible properties such as buildings and lands, intangible properties such as royalty incomes from books, oil wells, and music scores or lyrics, and other passive income streams. These amounts may be quite substantial, and if the person inheriting is too young, they may not know how to deal with it. If they are immature spiritually, emotional, or physically, they may squander the inherited wealth within a few years because they have no appreciation for the hard-earned wealth and have received too much in too short a time.

I have seen many young people dwindle their inherited wealth in just a few years. They acquire horrible and destructive personal habits that result in a rapid deterioration of all that valuable wealth. I have also seen people who have treated their inheritances with a great deal of respect and responsibility. They have used those proceedings for constructive causes, especially those that reflect God's wonderful love for underprivileged children, orphans, widows, the poor, the disadvantaged, mentally and physically challenged, battered women, abused children, and cancer and AIDS patients. Such inheritors are full of Christ's love for others. They serve to make others happy even when it means much personal sacrifice on their part.

An inheritance is a great blessing to receive if you are fortunate, but you should invest this inheritance with a proper mindset.

In summarizing this chapter, it is important to reinforce the following truths:

1. Money is a good blessing from God, but if it's not used properly with the right attitude, it can become a source of conflict in a family, especially between husband and wife.

2. There are at least ten principles that can be applied to manage wealth successfully. These are practical in nature, and they have worked well for more than fifty years for my family.

3. The most important guiding truth to remember in managing your finances is to note that all you earn is God's. All your wealth belongs to Him. You are merely a caretaker and not an owner. Whatever wealth you invest in your life presently will affect your happiness and joy while you are alive, and it will affect the happiness, joy, and positive value of the generations that follow.

4. Finances are like a dynamite. They can be destructive or constructive, depending upon how they are used. When your ultimate purpose is to magnify God—who gave you all your wealth from your hard work and from what's inherited from your dear ones—you will discover financial management is a great tool to bring joy and fulfillment to your family and to countless others in your community, your country, and your world.

5. When we earn money the honest way—because we're obedient to God's wisdom—we can feel fulfillment from the hard-earned earnings. Quick money, earned in unethical or illegal ways, is at risk of losing it all: "Wealth gained by dishonesty will be diminished. But he who gathers by labor will increase" (Proverbs 13:11).

Disclaimer: I am not a licensed financial planner or advisor. I strongly recommend using one as I have done myself for many decades. My suggestions in this chapter are primarily from my personal experience of fifty plus years of managing our family finances.

Three Actions I Can Take for One Month after Reading This
Chapter

1.
2.
3.

Chapter Nine
TIME MANAGEMENT

To everything there is a season. A time for
every purpose under heaven.
—ECCLESIASTES 3:1

Because of laziness the building decays. And
through idleness of hands the house leaks.
—ECCLESIASTES 10:18

Time Shockers

This chapter will open with some shocking statistics about the way we use our time.

Assuming on average, we live seventy years, we have a total of 613,200 hours (70 years x 365 days/year x 24 hours/day), or 36,792,000 minutes in our time bank. The way we spend these millions of precious minutes determines the value we have added to ourselves, our families and friends, our countries, and our world. Of course, we generally sleep for one-third of our lives, which is 204,400 hours (613,000/3), or 12,264,000 minutes.

In America, we enter workforce after graduation from a university at twenty-two and retire at sixty-five, and we work full-time at least forty hours per week. Thus, we work 43 years x 52 weeks/year x 40 hours/week = 89,440 hours. During this working period, we are *supposed* to be productive for eight hours per day, but my research and that of other productivity experts indicates that we engage in productive time for only about six hours per day, thus wasting two hours per day or 25 percent of our workweek, which is nearly 22,360 hours (89,440 x 25 percent) of our working lives. Further, if we consider the fact that nearly 20 percent of what we do is ineffective or unnecessary, we can add another 17,888 hours of unproductive time to our working lives. In all, then, during the forty-three years of our work life, we're likely to squander 40,248 hours (22,360 + 17,888). Thus, our inefficient time utilization in our lives is 40,248 / 89,440 = 0.45, which is 45 percent.

Now, during the one-third of our lives when we are supposed to refresh our minds and bodies through recreation, we engage ourselves in passive recreation rather than active recreation. When I was a boy and a young man, I played soccer and other sports with my friends. We developed our mental capabilities to play like a team, toughen our bodies physically, and nursed bleeding knees and toes. Nowadays, most young boys and men sit at a computer or in front of a TV, watching somebody else playing sports. That's passive recreation. That might not be a good characterization, but too many young people and adults are actively pursuing passive recreation. Is it any wonder that there are so many couch potatoes, adding unnecessary obesity to their waists and increasing their chances for heart disease and diabetes.

On a very conservative basis, if we assume about one hour per day of passive recreation, that is equivalent to 60 years x 365 days/year x 1 hour/day = 21,900 hours from the age of ten to seventy. If we add up all the non-value-adding time of our lives, it amounts to 40,248 + 21,900 = 62,148 hours from age ten to seventy. That's about seven years (62,148 / (365 x 24)). Even though we live an average of seventy years, we each are adding value to ourselves and to humanity for only sixty-three years.

Taking this one step further, the 7.9 billion of us in the world are going to potentially waste nearly fifty-five billion person-years during our lifetimes.

Time Is Irreversible

Certain things may be retracted or taken back, but time is irreversible. Every precious minute we spend is gone forever. We've either invested that minute in a value-adding activity or cause or wasted it, never to be recovered.

If little drops make the ocean, little minutes make hours, many hours make several days, and many days make many years. This ought to shock us about our ineffectiveness and bring home the most important point, which is that every minute of our lives must be viewed as precious God-given time to help ourselves and our fellow humans. Simply put, we must learn how to manage our minutes.

Two Common Misconceptions about Using Time

During my worldwide interactions with people from different educational, professional, social, economic, political, and religious backgrounds, I have been fascinated and terribly surprised by the extent of their misconceptions about time:

Time Is Ours

In several countries, many people in the villages and rural areas think that time is at their disposal. For them, arriving at a wedding reception an hour late is not a big deal. In fact, some people think that the later they arrive, the more important they'll be perceived to be. Dignitaries rarely come to such events on time in these cultures.

This attitude that time is ours misses one important biblical truth: God is the ultimate controller of time and space. When we realize that time is not under our control—because God is in control—we should pay closer attention to natural and human-made disasters. Sadly, the horrific human disaster of December 24, 2004—the massive tsunami, resulting in more than 240,000 people perishing—brought home this point. Before that fateful tsunami reached the shores of Sri Lanka, there was about a three-hour window to evacuate. Since people didn't react until they saw it, and then it was too close and too powerful to escape. For whatever reason, adequate tsunami detectors and sensors were not installed between Indonesia and Sri Lanka. If the tragedy of the tsunami taught us any lessons about time, maybe we should be careful not to ignore the value of time when preparing for a future tsunami.

The attitude that "time is ours" has a more deadly underlying disease: *complacency*. Individuals, families, companies, and countries suffer from this horrible problem of becoming complacent.

Time Is Money

At the other extreme of the first misconception about time; this one claims that time must be treated like money. Unfortunately, in the postmodern thinking of our era where there are very few absolutes to hold on to, individuals have ruined their marriages, companies have become greedy, and everything has become like a money machine when time has been "converted" to dollars. Wage rates are expressed in dollars per hour, TV commercials are priced as dollars per minute—or even per second—and lawyers, psychiatrists, and consultants are compensated based on dollars per billable hour or billable minute.

Sometimes, I hear parents tell their children, "I'm too busy now, honey. Can we *schedule* five minutes to talk later tonight?" Some parents are treating time as money to such an extent that their children are like an intrusion in their to-do lists. Eastern societies have not fallen into this trap yet, but that's changing for the worse rapidly because of an imbalanced use of information, technology, and social media.

It is relevant to say time is money in a business context, especially where revenues are literally based on time. Let's not drag that adage into our family lives and mess them up even more than we already have.

For me, time is respect. When we value every precious minute, we're basically valuing God-given opportunities to add value to every passing moment for His honor and glory. When we say we will start a lecture at a particular time, we mustn't waste one minute beyond that. If I walk into the classroom one minute late, I'm basically saying, "I don't care you've had to wait for me." If there are fifty students in that class, in essence, fifty minutes of their time collectively is wasted. If a student comes into class two minutes late, it may not a be big deal for them, but if forty-nine other students turn around to see this student entering the classroom, they have possibly distracted themselves from a very important point I was making. If it takes another two or three minutes for that student to settle down, we have collectively wasted 250 person-minutes of precious time.

I have some very interesting rules in my classes for arriving later than the scheduled start time. I enforce these rules out of respect to my students and their valuable time and not because of my authority as a teacher. I have all kinds of bonus points when the entire class is on time. During the fall of 2005, my nearly fifty students in Statistics came on time for three successive lectures, which is a record in fifty years of teaching.

The Ten Common Time Stressors

Managing time effectively and efficiently requires knowing which types of activities are effective and which types of activities can be done efficiently. To swat a mosquito on your nose, you'd normally use your palm and not a sledgehammer because the palm has just enough pressure to kill the mosquito without crushing your nose, you don't need to search for a sledgehammer when it takes a fraction of that time to extend your palm, and you don't want to smash your nose.

I have watched people stress out unnecessarily because they are doing the wrong things very efficiently. This statement applies to corporations and individuals. So much daily stress can be avoided most of the time. The smart thing to do is to recognize when we are about to do things. There are things you must do lest they stress you out, and there is no choice to not do them even though they increase your stress. However, there are ways to anticipate such situations ahead of time and deal with them efficiently. I call these situations "time stressors." The most common ones include the following:

1. mornings (usually between six and nine)
2. evenings (usually between five and seven)
3. serious or prolonged illness of close family members or friends
4. marital issues
5. teenage years (for those experiencing them and those watching them)
6. large parties at home
7. extremely painful and sad occasions in life (separations, divorce, loss of health and wealth, and death in the family, especially a sudden death)
8. frequent travel, long-distance travel, and vacations
9. preparing for tests or exams
10. first-time events in life (job interviews, blind dates, bungee jumping, class attendance, hiking, skydiving, flying, swimming, driving, driving on highways, hurricanes or cyclones, earthquakes, fires, tornadoes, tsunamis, fires, and plane crashes)

There are effective methods for managing time stressors:

1. Expect that you may be stressed.
2. Pray and submit the anxiety to God.
3. Trust, like a child, that God will enable you to encounter the time stressor.
4. Identify the benefits of handling the time stressors.

On June 26, 2000, it was time to attend the funeral services for our youngest son. Paul had been hit by an illegal driver three days earlier and killed at just twenty years old.

On the morning of June 26, I spent some time expecting the intensity of the emotional pain our family was going to experience. I knelt and prayed to my Lord, asking him to grant His extraordinary strength to cope with the heart-wrenching event. I trusted Him to do so, recalling His Words: "Be still and Know that I am God" (Psalm 46:10) and "I will never leave you nor forsake you" (Hebrews 13:5). I said, "God, how do you expect me to actually see the good that can come out of this horrific tragedy? 'All things work together for good to them that love God, and to those who are the called according to His purpose'" (Romans 8:28). It was painfully difficult. I certainly didn't know what good was going to come when such a young life had been taken so suddenly. Yet, I had to say to myself, "I don't know now, but I'm sure God will show me how His promise in Romans 8:28 is still true."

Looking back now, the events of June 23 and June 26, 2000, changed my life completely. After thirteen months of agonizing prayers, the Lord gave me a ministry call, first on a part-time basis in May 2001 and then on a full-time basis on February 9, 2006. As a result of this ministry, we started taking many underprivileged children from impoverished areas in India and providing them with food, clothing, and education. A large percentage of these precious children are orphans and slum dwellers. Since 2001, we've had the privilege of graduating more than twenty thousand children from tenth grade, which is when they become eligible to be gainfully employed. We support several orphans in Honduras and Colombia and built nine worship centers in India. Today, more than 1,500 people worship God in secure and comfortable places. Nearly five thousand pastors have been trained in my productivity management principles to increase their effectiveness and efficiency for God's resources. The ministry has been able to present the good news of hope to thousands of people in several countries.

Today, we have learned two important truths from our son's homegoing:

1. Our children are God's first—and only then are they ours. We are merely God's stewards of our children. We raise them according to His paths and precepts. He loves our children more than we can, and He created them (Genesis 1:26–27).
2. God's promises never fail because He is *always* trustworthy. Romans 8:28 is always true for His children.

Time Is Life

If we internalize this phrase, we'd have a very different perspective in time management. It takes a fraction of a second for a catastrophic event to occur. However, it also takes that much time for a positive epiphany, discovery, invention, or trillion-dollar idea to come. Time transcends our lives. Every minute must be used wisely to contribute to our lives. We are the stewards of time because we're the stewards of the lives God has granted us. Realizing that time is life improves our lives significantly.

The Nine Time Management Principles

The following principles can help you manage your time more productively. They are not listed in order of importance. They are not exhaustive, but they represent the most practical and most results-oriented principles.

The MIMU Principle (Task Priority)

We have many tasks to complete every day, but if we have to complete all of them, we'll be stressed out. Prioritizing tasks is essential.

Work on most important and most urgent (MIMU) tasks first.

Traditional thinking says that the busier you are, the better you are using your time. This is a common fallacy because we may be working extremely hard on the least important and the least urgent (LILU) tasks. Most individuals in families and enterprises are guilty of doing LILU tasks efficiently, but their effectiveness is zero. One way to prioritize is to identify each task by A, B, C. "A" items are MIMU, "B" items are MU, and "C" items are LILU.

In 2008, a laser procedure was set to be done on my *right* eye. After the ophthalmologist wrote up my procedure and sent me down to the operation room, a medical technician marked my *left* eye for the surgery. He was thinking that my left eye was to his *right*, and that's the one he marked. This was an extremely dangerous mistake. Fortunately, I stopped this dangerous situation immediately and called for the surgeon before I had the procedure done on the wrong eye. His effectiveness, zero!

The Duty Principle (Handling Crises)

Never delegate tasks that are your duty, thinking you will save time. You can delegate all other tasks—but not the ones that are perceived to be your duties.

When major natural disasters and national tragedies occur, the highest government official will usually visit the place and the affected people because they represent the entire country when the people need reassurance. Queen Elizabeth II appeared publicly when Princess Diana was killed in a car accident, and President George W. Bush put his arms around a fireman when terrorists brought down the Twin Towers on 9/11.

If a member of a church passes away, the senior pastor—the highest-ranking official in the church—must not delegate his duty to someone else to visit the family when he is in town or say, "I'm sorry. I am extremely busy preparing for my sermon next Sunday."

The Delegation Principle (People-Building)

Delegate every task that you don't need to do. Let those tasks that don't need your expertise, skill, or time be done by someone else. This might be easier said than done, especially if you don't like to delegate. You may think delegation is passing the buck to someone else (see chapter 7).

Delegating is an effective way to build people up. When we delegate, we help people develop self-confidence, feel empowered, and take on more responsibilities. By delegating properly, using the MDF formula, we can accomplish more of the MIMU items. Moses was taught the principle of delegation by his father-in-law, Jethro, which enabled Moses to use his precious time wisely and preserve his health.

An excellent manager delegates to develop their people. This is called "people-building."

Overriding the Planning Principle (Relational Priority)

When necessary, in relationships with your dear family and close friends, you may have to override these principles. Otherwise, you'll be expending more time and energy fixing the problems we created by ignoring our relationships with family and close friends.

Effectiveness is the degree of accomplishment of relevant objectives. If nine of the ten objectives you wish to accomplish in a year are relevant, your effectiveness is 90 percent. For more discussion on effectiveness, see *Total Productivity Management.*

For example, it's your wedding anniversary, and your spouse calls you at the office, asking you to come home an hour early. Even if you have a relatively important meeting at that time, explain the situation and try to move the meeting to another day or time. Most of the time, your request will be honored—and your spouse will be very pleased. A simple gesture like this may seem to take away your time at work, but it's worth it. A happy spouse makes a happy executive—and a happy executive makes a happy enterprise.

Jesus went to a wedding in Cana, considering it an opportunity to minister. His mother, Mary, asked Him to do something about the wine running out. He did His first miracle of His ministry to an utter joy of the wedding host (John 2:1–10).

The Balance Principle

In all natural systems, balance is an important prerequisite for effectiveness, efficiency, and productivity. While practicing time management, it is necessary to follow the balance principle, which says, "Balance managing time for total productivity and not partial productivity."

This principle can save billions of dollars for enterprises because more than 80 percent of the time, for-profit companies and not-for-profit educational institutions suboptimize their resource utilization by devoting their attention to increasing efficiency of human effort by using partial productivity measures, such as output per man-hour. Except for in a few entities, labor does not account for the largest portion of resources. Materials, energy, machines, equipment, buildings, and working capital account for as much as 90 percent. The total productivity measure must be the focus since it considers the simultaneous utilization of all resources, including labor. I have devoted more than fifty years of my professional life to researching, teaching, and implementing this measure (see Sumanth 1984, McGraw-Hill; and 1998, CRC Press/Taylor and Francis).

The Mutual Respect Principle (Trustworthiness)

Quite often, family members hurt each other emotionally by using words we don't mean. We disrespect the ones we love and care about deeply. I have seen the importance of this principle in my own marriage of fifty years. Many times, I tended not to show respect to my wife because of my ego, superiority complex, and positions as father and husband. I failed to understand that when you respect others, they will respect you. This is so obvious, yet how often have wonderful marriages broken apart because couples did not practice the Golden Rule that Jesus taught: "Do unto others as you would want others to do unto you" (Matthew 7:12).

More than sixty years ago, IBM became one of the first companies in the world to use mutual respect as one of its core values. Today, many companies do. Making a conscious effort to show mutual respect with family members will result in many positive outcomes, including harmony, peace, joy, stability, endurance, and flexibility. Using this principle can save tons of precious time and resources.

The Significance Principle (Beyond Success)

Solomon was the son of King David, the wisest and wealthiest king in the world at his time (approximately 2,900 years ago). He wrote more than three thousand proverbs (see the book of Proverbs) and other literature about wisdom, including the book of Ecclesiastes and the Song of Solomon.

Solomon had three phases in his spiritual life: his God-fearing, pagan-loving, and God-acknowledging phases. In his second phase, he offered many wise statements, which characterized what he called "life under the sun." In fact, he used this phrase twenty-nine times in Ecclesiastes. The phrase "under the sun" is important because Solomon set out to experiment with what would happen outside of or apart from the revelation of God. Fortunately, he concludes the book with God's revelation that fearing God and keeping His commandments should be the goal of all humans. Otherwise, "all is vanity," and there will be "vexation of the spirit." Toiling in amassing wealth, wisdom, popularity, honor, and diligence leads to meaningless effort. Success is temporary at best, and it results ultimately in futility and dissatisfaction.

When trying to manage time, remember that vanity (meaningless) and vexation of the spirit (confusion, depression, and bewilderment) lead to no significance. I suggest using the significance principle, which says: "In everything we do, let's *first* seek significance, then success *always* follows. But seeking success does *not* guarantee significance."

The Consistency Principle (Diligence)

"It is better to be good consistently than to be perfect occasionally in every sphere of life, especially in time management." Significance is a rational goal in life for true believer. It seeks to please God and live in the short term and long term for Him and to fulfill His purpose for our lives.

Humans do not, by nature, like consistency because it's difficult. We seek consistency in critical-performance situations, such as ensuring that the landing gear deploys every time the pilot lands the plane. In less critical situations, such as retail customer service, we experience inconsistency, mediocrity, and indifference for the most part. Japanese cars, cameras, and watches have such high value because they meet and/or exceed customer expectations every time; they've perfected the art and science of consistency.

Consistency in everything, including time management, requires self-discipline. Unfortunately, many people lack self-discipline. Consistency does not mean lacking creativity and innovation. In fact, we must be consistent in creativity *and* innovation.

If we adopt a certain method for managing our time for a particular period, but we decide to change that method, we must use the new method consistently until we replace it with a better one. During the COVID pandemic, we had to change our worship in the church from in-person attendance to an online format. This reduced the time driving to and from church and costs, but we are back to in-person attendance at church now. We need to be consistent to have meaningful worship experiences and fellowship with our fellow believers.

The Reworking Principle (Minimizing Wastefulness)

"Do it right the first time" is the underlying concept behind this principle because if we leave a job not done according to the specified instructions, the results are likely to be substandard. We will have to do the job again or discard it. There will be negative consequences in the future—maybe even after we die. Redoing a job always takes more time, and it is boring and disinteresting. More time results in higher costs.

In a family environment, we build relationships consistently and strive to improve their quality, authenticity, and genuineness. In the process, we create relational defects. To rectify them, we must expend energy, time, and other valuable resources.

When your teenager talks back to you, you feel insulted and might say something that's harsh or unreasonable, which can damage the child's self-worth and self-esteem. The emotional wounds from these experiences could remain for life. Mending this issue may take years. The emotional damage may manifest in self-destructive behaviors, which no good parent wants.

"Do it right the first time" when managing your time and your relationships. An emotionally wounded family member is a liability to society. By minimizing the relational defects, we can build a stronger community of humans around the world.

When we keep God at the center of our lives, we follow His Word and please Him. It will be natural in "whatever we do, to do it heartily as to the Lord, and not to people" (Colossians 3:23). When we please God, we are doing our best.

Being consistent is one of the most difficult behaviors in life. It affects being married, raising children to be valuable citizens, managing employees and associates, leading organizations, managing political philosophies, and managing countries.

Three Actions I Can Take for One Month after Reading This Chapter

1.
2.
3.

Chapter Ten
LEADERSHIP IN THE FAMILY

Lead me in Your truth and teach me.
—PSALM 25:5

All organizational systems, including human groups, animal groups, and bird groups, have leaders. The silverback gorilla is most often the leader of a group of gorillas, a rooster is the leader of a bunch of hens, and a male lion is the leader of a pride. The alpha male is the leader of a wolf pack, and a herd of elephants has a matriarch. A chief executive officer or a chairperson of a company is its leader. Likewise, every family unit has a leader.

Great leaders in the Bible include Noah, Abraham, Joseph, Moses, Joshua, Deborah, Daniel, Esther, David, Nehemiah, Peter, Paul, and James. These leaders share some common traits:

> reverence for God
> obedience to God
> faith in God
> perseverance for God's purposes
> appointed or chosen by God

I didn't mention God, Jesus Christ, or the Holy Spirit as leaders because they are the Triune God (three persons of the same Godhead).

They created these human leaders, and it would be sacrilegious to put them on the same level as human leaders.

If we emulate these biblical leaders in our own families, we will be so much better off as mothers, fathers, grandparents, great-grandparents, husbands, wives, sons, daughters, sons-in-law, and daughters-in-law.

Leadership Styles of Famous Biblical Leaders

Noah was an obedient, quiet, determined, and patient leader. When God told him to build a mammoth-sized ark, it took him 120 years—but did not succumb to the ridicule of the people around him. He heard God's directive and followed it with a tenacity of purpose that few can imagine or demonstrate.

Noah literally implemented every specification God gave him to build the ark, including materials, sizes, shapes, and selection of animals to go into it. Only his immediate family was chosen by God to be in the ark. The rest of the people perished because of their rebellion against God. Noah was a man of great integrity to God, and he showed his steadfastness to his faith while building the ark (Genesis 6:8–10:32).

Abraham epitomized faith in God and faithfulness to God. He was born and brought up in the land of Ur (present-day Iraq) and worshipped pagan gods. When God called him (Genesis 12:1–3), he left his family, blindly followed where God promised, and did what he was asked to do. In fact, when God asked him to sacrifice his son, Isaac, he didn't think for a moment that he wouldn't have lineage from Isaac if he did what God asked him to do. God saw his blind faith, and at the last moment—when Abraham took up his knife to sacrifice Isaac—God stopped him. He rewarded Abram (calling him Abraham) with His covenant (Genesis 12:3) that he would be the father of all nations and that his descendants would be like the stars of heaven and granules of uncountable sand. During his lifetime, he wouldn't be able to reach the Promised Land, but his descendants would. Throughout his life, Abraham demonstrated integrity of heart and loyalty to God and to his family (Genesis 3–45).

Joseph was a dreamer and a favorite son of his father, Jacob (who was renamed Israel), which attracted the envy of his brothers. The brothers threw Joseph into a pit and sold him to the Midianites as they were going to Egypt. They told a huge lie to their father and said that Joseph had been attacked by an animal and killed.

Through further providential events, including an attempted seduction by Potiphar's wife, Joseph ran from the temptation. He was falsely accused of rape and was put in prison. God drew Pharaoh's favor toward Joseph and made him the prime minister of Egypt—second in power only to Pharaoh. Joseph had many leadership traits:

1. reverence to God and His precepts
2. loyalty to Potiphar
3. godly wisdom to interpret Pharaoh's dream
4. wise forecast of the famine, as revealed by God
5. forgiveness of his brothers and magnanimity to them
6. care toward his father, Jacob, during his last part of life
7. favor with God and Pharaoh
8. integrity with Pharaoh, his brothers, and his father (Exodus 2–40; Leviticus 1–27; Numbers 1–36; Deuteronomy 1–34)

Moses also had many leadership traits:

1. humility
2. meekness
3. unwavering allegiance to God
4. holiness (to the point of being allowed by God to see Him partially)
5. God's favor (to be able to talk to God)
6. performing God's miracles
7. writing the laws of God
8. leading the Israelites through a forty-year wilderness journey (Joshua 1–24)

Joshua followed Moses's leadership and was an obedient and faithful follower of God and Moses, his mentor, for decades. His leadership traits include the following:

1. courage to explore unknown territory at Moses's request, along with Caleb
2. loyalty to God ("As for me and my house, we shall serve the Lord" (Joshua 24:15).
3. obedience to God's instructions (he was asked to march into Jericho with drums and no weapons)
4. integrity of heart to God, to His people Israel, and to Rahab (Judges 4:1–5:31)

Deborah, the only female judge of Israel, showed courage, faithfulness to God, and integrity.

Daniel served in the administrations of the Babylonian and Persian kings. He was in his teens when he was exiled to Babylon in 605 BC by King Nebuchadnezzar. He rose to the highest position under Nebuchadnezzar, who respected Daniel's favor with God and his godly wisdom to interpret his dreams. Daniel was thrown into a lion's den for not bowing and worshipping Nebuchadnezzar's statue, but God delivered him by closing the lions' mouths.

Daniel's leadership traits included the following:

1. allegiance to God first and always
2. godly wisdom
3. purity of thought, mind, and action
4. courage (not to count the cost of obedience to God)
5. integrity
6. diplomacy

Esther, an extraordinary Jewish girl, was adopted by her uncle Mordecai when she was in exile under the Persian king, Ahasuerus, who ruled 127 provinces from India to Ethiopia (Esther 1:1). Through God's providence, she replaced Vashti, the first queen of Ahasuerus, when a decree was passed by the king through the sinister plot of Haman to destroy Mordecai. Mordecai sent a message to Queen Esther to remind of her responsibility, as a Jew, to speak to the king and prevent Haman's plot from annihilating the Jews. Mordecai appealed to Esther's conscience about her privilege and said, "Yet who knows whether you have come to the kingdom for such a time as this?" (Esther 4:14). Esther asked all the Jews in Shushan (located in present-day Iran) to fast and pray for her and her maids so that she could muster enough courage to appear before the king: "And so I will go to the King, which is against the law, and if I perish, I perish" (Esther 4:16).

She risked her life, went to the king, and invited him for a banquet at her palace. After a series of events, Esther saved her people, and Haman was sent to the gallows, which he had set up for Mordecai (Esther 7:10).

Esther demonstrated many leadership qualities:

1. deep commitment and loyalty to her people
2. courage to do the right thing even when her life was in danger
3. intelligence to communicate with her king
4. integrity
5. trust in God and His power
6. recognition of the power of intercessory fasting prayers

About three thousand years ago, David ruled all the twelve tribes of Israel for forty years (1 Samuel 16–31; 2 Samuel 1–24; 1 Kings 1–2:10). He is known as the greatest king of Israel of all time, and his leadership traits included the following:

1. devotion to God
2. loyalty to God and his soldiers
3. respect to God's anointed servants
4. not committing the same sin twice
5. magnanimity
6. being a man of his word

7. integrity
8. courage
9. genuine repentance

David did not forget about Shimei's cursing when he was fleeing from his rebellious son, Absalom. He was human in this regard, but for the most part, he was a noble man.

Nehemiah (Nehemiah 1–13) was an extraordinary leader. It's not surprising that sermons and Christian books on leadership often refer to his capable leadership in rebuilding the walls of Jerusalem with King Artaxerxes' permission. He, as a trusted cupbearer to the king, accomplished some extraordinary things for the people of Jerusalem. Nehemiah's leadership traits included the following:

1. burden for his homeland
2. intensive prayer
3. trust in God
4. trustworthy
5. diplomatic
6. strategic planning
7. tenacity of purpose
8. wisdom to discern distraction
9. fear of God
10. primary dependence on God
11. integrity

Nehemiah's rebuilding project was completed in a remarkably short period of fifty-two days. Founding pastor, Satish Kumar, deriving inspiration from this record time, built his Calvary Temple church in Hyderabad, India in fifty-two days.

Peter (Matthew, Mark, Luke, John, and Acts 1:15–5:42; 1 Peter and 2 Peter) was a uniquely chosen disciple of Jesus Christ as the one to build His church (Matthew 16:18). Peter, though a fisherman, was encouraged by Jesus to promise him that he would be one of the "fishers of men."

Peter's leadership traits are a study by itself, but for the purpose of this chapter's focus on leadership, here are his prominent leadership traits:

1. integrity of heart toward his Master, Jesus
2. courage in persecution even to the Crucifixion
3. enduring suffering
4. humility in Jesus's presence
5. impetuosity about his belief and faith
6. loyalty to God
7. natural leadership
8. out-of-the-box thinking
9. seeking the common good of the church

Paul's leadership in planting churches was amazing. He founded the church in Thessalonica (in present-day Greece) after preaching for just three Sabbaths there. His life was one of contrasts between highly intellectual, influential Pharisee to a humble sufferer for his Master, Jesus Christ, after his conversion on the road to Damascus.

Paul wrote twelve of the twenty-seven books of the New Testament—more than any other single author of the New Testament. His passion and dedication for serving his Lord was extraordinary, resulting ultimately in his martyrdom by crucifixion (Acts 9:1–31; 11:19–30; 12:25–28:31; Romans 1:1; Philemon). Among all the apostles, he is my spiritual role model. His leadership traits include the following:

1. absolute allegiance to his Master
2. brilliant apologetic
3. exemplary in walking the talk
4. extraordinary spiritual and physical endurance in sufferings
5. extremely caring of his mentees
6. humility par excellence
7. integrity of heart toward his Master, Jesus
8. natural leadership
9. total commitment to the purpose he was called for

James (James 1–5) was the stepbrother of Jesus. He was an influential leader of the Jerusalem church. He was a man of great spiritual wisdom and pragmatism. His epistle, James, reflects that. In fact, some consider this epistle "wisdom literature," but it's more often described as a diatribe (a writing style intended to move the reader to action). He became Jesus's follower after His death, but as a sibling of the Master, he was respected among the founding members of the Jerusalem church. His notable leadership traits include

1. unshakable faith in, and commitment to, a doctrinally sound early church,
2. statesmanlike,
3. pragmatic wisdom, and
4. integrity of heart toward God.

The Seven Common Characteristics of Good to Great Leaders

The brief narratives of the above-mentioned individuals of the Bible give us some common characteristics of great leaders. How do we apply them to leadership in our families? First and foremost, the husband and wife must demonstrate devotion to God, acceptance, and followship of His precepts.

Second, they must lead by example. Children emulate their parents more in their actions than their words.

Third, both parents must love God first and love each other and their children next.

Fourth, the father must set the tone for moral leadership at home. He and his wife must have their individual prayers and family prayers. They must consistently teach their children to have daily devotions. A family that prays together stays together.

Fifth, the parents must demonstrate leadership in stewardship. This would automatically require tithing and offering time, talents, and other resources they've been blessed with. Children growing up in such a family environment will try their best to manage all they've been given, including responsibility.

Sixth, good "leader-parents" will raise good leader-parents. Such replication is necessary to perpetuate family values and to create sustainable families.

Seventh, parents must adopt appropriate leadership postures, depending upon the stages of growth of their children, under different circumstances. One glove doesn't fit all.

All leaders have some managerial roles to fulfill, but not all managers are good leaders. Parents must pray before they even think that God will enable them to be effective leaders once they get married and have children. Leadership is special.

Three Actions I Can Take for One Month after Reading This Chapter

1.
2.
3.

Chapter Eleven

PRINCIPLES OF FAMILY MANAGEMENT

Some general principles can be gleaned from the sixty-six books of the Bible and applied successfully to managing families. I will present these time-tested principles under the following four subheadings:

1. For the Father and Husband
2. For the Mother and Wife
3. For the Children and Grandchildren
4. For the In-Laws

For the Father and Husband

In Ephesians, apostle Paul asks the husbands to "love their wives just as Christ also loved the church and gave himself for her" (Ephesians 5:25). Further, Paul tells husbands to "love their own wives as their own bodies" and that "he who loves his wife loves himself" (Ephesians 5:28). Paul also alludes to Genesis 2:24 when he tells the husband to "leave his father and mother and be joined to his wife, and the two shall become one flesh" (Ephesians 5:31).

Husbands and fathers have a tough role to play in family management. When the children are young, fathers enjoy their time with them. They play with them, teach them as many things as they can, adore them for any accomplishment, and generally show patience with them. When the kids grow into adolescents, problems seem to begin when boys tend to show resentment because they're told no to certain requests, which are often influenced by their peers.

Fathers tend to assert their positional leadership and be authoritative in many situations to ensure quick communication with their youngsters. If the father doesn't show empathetic love and shuts off communication, the youngster obeys the father in the short term, but he wants to get out of the house and live on his own as soon as he can. The unresolved resentment often stays into adulthood—and even after becoming a parent himself. As a compensatory behavior, this parent gives more freedom to his son—so much so that the son may be overly pampered and not learn responsible behavior. A father is in a learning mode with his first child, and he eases up a bit with the second one. The first child can become envious of his sibling if he's being treated differently. Favoritism can have long-term negative consequences. God warns against favoritism because He does not show partiality. Therefore, fathers, as they love God and strive to become like their Master, should avoid favorite treatment of one child to the detriment of the others.

Fathers tend to be gentler toward their daughters. Many daughters become "relational shock absorbers" between their fathers and mothers and between their fathers and brothers. The relational bond is established between a mother and her baby when the latter is in her womb; nine months of the physical bond is a unique factor for mothers. It's no wonder that most children tend to go to their mothers when they're in a quandary. When grown-up football players are paying homage, they generally yell, "Hi, Mom. I love you!" But when it comes to learning many responsibilities, young men think of their fathers. Fathers and mothers are created with equal importance and self-worth by God. Their roles are differently set because God, in His wisdom, knows how to bring complementary skills from the father and the mother to develop the family into productive individuals.

The apostle Paul gives another important instruction to fathers: "And you fathers, do not provoke your children to wrath, but bring them up in the training and admonition of the Lord" (Ephesians 6:4). Interestingly, Paul gives this instruction only to the father and not to the mother. Clearly, God knew when He created man and woman that the man usually has more ego than the woman. It's generally more natural for a man to stand his ground more readily than the woman. Because of this tendency, fathers can feel their authority is being threatened when a child retaliates. Patience is a virtue, and men need a higher dosage of it in conflicting scenarios.

David was a great king, but he was a poor father. He did not correct his eldest son, Amnon, when his daughter Tamar was raped by her stepbrother, Amnon. David was scared of his son, Absalom, and fled from his palace when Absalom plotted to overthrow his legitimate father-king. At an individual level, he was a "beloved of God," but David did not raise all his sons to be like him in devotion to Yahweh, the God of Israel. Of course, part of the reason for not disciplining his sons was because he did not have the moral courage, recalling his adultery with the married woman, Bathsheba, and his plotting to have her husband, Uriah, killed in a battle.

Samuel was a righteous man all his life, but he did not train his two sons to be righteous. In fact, his sons were so wicked that God pronounced death on them. To some extent, Jacob's partiality toward his son Joseph resulted in his brothers being intensely jealous of him.

All we see in King Saul's relationship with his son Jonathan is pettiness, jealousy, and hatred against his very dear friend David. What a poor example of nobility in the first king of Israel.

In first-century Christendom, the apostle Paul is a good example of an unmarried father figure. Paul's adopted child, Timothy, was groomed by him as an excellent example of godliness, empathy, and devotion to God. Paul cared for and nurtured his protégé. He also groomed other young men—Silas, Titus, Aristarchus, and Tychicus—among many others.

Biological and adoptive fathers can be successful in influencing their children by practicing as many of the following principles as possible.

1. Love your wife as Christ loves her as the bride of the church. Everything follows from this.
2. Treat all your children equally—without favoritism—just as God does not show partiality.
3. Love your children consistently.
4. Do not be afraid of correcting your children when they're detouring from godly paths. Correct them with love and point out the negative consequences of their wrong choices.
5. Start teaching biblical values from infancy and practice what you preach.
6. Show tough love to children consistently.
7. Do not take sides with your wife unless you see the wisdom in doing so.
8. Always pray for your wife and children. Be in a state of prayer for them throughout the day.
9. Always cushion correction between affirmation and encouragement (the sandwich formula) when dealing with conflict-prone situations.
10. Teach your children to make Jesus Christ their best friend.
11. Remind your family that you, your wife, and all your children must love God more than each other and yourselves.
12. Let your children know they're precious in God's sight and in your sight. Let them feel beyond a doubt that they're always welcome in your home.
13. Do not provoke your children to wrath; instead, bring them up in the training and admonition of the Lord.

For the Mother and Wife

The apostle Paul instructs mothers and wives as he did with fathers and husbands:

> Submit to your own husbands as to the Lord, for the husband is the head of the wife as also Christ is head of the church; and He is the Savior of the body. Therefore, just as the church is subject to Christ, so let the wives be to their own husbands in everything. (Ephesians 5:22–24)

In the world we live in today, the word "submit" has a negative connotation. If we examine the full context, however, we see that Paul was asking for mutual submission: "submitting to one another in the fear of God" (Ephesians 5:21). Is the intent of this submission to put one another's needs before the other?

Further, we see that the Greek word for "submit," *hupotasso*, means "to place under ordered relationships, especially when one submits to another." So, what did the apostle really mean? If we examine Paul's instruction, he's telling wives to submit to their husbands as they would to the Lord Jesus. When we accept Jesus as our Savior and Master, we should have no problem submitting to His authority. In fact, during the millennial kingdom on the earth, everyone will submit to His kingship.

To understand the concept of submission, we can use the term "yield." When we are driving on a highway ramp, merging with oncoming traffic, we yield to traffic and wait our turn. When we are waiting in a line at a store, we don't think of submitting to those ahead of us. We do not need to make a huge deal out of the fact that Paul was asking wives to submit to the leadership in the family. Until the late 1960s, we didn't have any issues with this term "submit" for the most part. *Father Knows Best* was a popular TV show, and if we have the same kind of mutual love and respect between husband and wife, our families could see more effectively operating again.

The young pastor Timothy, while outlining the many requirements for deacons, suggests that they're to be husbands of one wife and be reverent—and that the wife must be reverent (1 Timothy 3:8–11). Age-old wisdom says, "Give respect and take respect." Active listening requires respect and thoughtfulness to hear the other person carefully—and not just listening for the sake of quick hearing and not paying attention to the message.

Just as fathers and husbands can benefit from using proven principles from God through the Bible, mothers and wives can too:

1. Respect your husband and love him, especially in front of others. A man's ego flared up into anger when he was disrespected by his wife. Husbands can take criticism privately much better than publicly.
2. Treat all your children without favoritism.
3. Love your children consistently.
4. Do not be afraid to correct your children. Do not say, "I will tell your father when he comes home." Instead say, "Your father and I have the same mindset on this matter."
5. You, as the mother, are in a unique position to impart good values upon your child from the time they are in your womb. In fact, singing worship songs, reciting simple Bible verses, and saying loving things during pregnancy will go a long way toward shaping the right values.
6. Of course, practice what you preach at home. Girls tend to imitate their mothers' behaviors long after being out of college and in their married lives.
7. Pray. Pray. Pray. Keep on praying for your children—before they go to school, while they are in the school, and when they go to bed. You can never pray too much. Susanne Wesley had nineteen children, and two of them were the founders of Methodism (Charles Wesley and John Wesley). Susanna prayed for each one of her children every day.
8. Practice tough love with your children. Susanna Wesley and Ruth Graham were great examples of this.
9. Pray for your husband daily, and fast when the Lord leads you. My wife, Chaya, did that for seventy-five days once, and God brought me out of a prolonged memory crisis and depression.
10. Follow principles 9–12 for fathers and husbands.

For Children and Grandchildren

The Bible has a special place for children. They are "a heritage from the Lord" (Psalm 127:3). Jesus chided His disciples when they obstructed the children from coming to Him. He said, "Let the little children come to Me, and do not forbid them" (Matthew 19:14). When we receive Jesus into our lives, He gives us "the right to become children of God" (John 1:12). The apostle John reiterated this: "Beloved, now we are children of God" (1 John 3:2).

In an earthly family, children help form and strengthen the biological bond between the husband and wife and the father and mother. Once again, the apostle Paul gave specific instructions to this important part of the family:

> Children, obey your parents in the Lord, for this is right. Honor your father and mother which is the first commandment with promise: that it may go well with you, and you may live long on the earth. (Ephesians 6:1–3)

The following principles help children become productive participants in the world—from childhood to adolescence:

1. Love God first and then your parents, guardians, and grandparents.
2. Respect your parents, guardians, grandparents, and teachers. Without respecting your teachers, it's difficult to receive the full knowledge that teachers are eager to impart to their pupils.
3. Plan your schoolwork carefully and prepare diligently for each day of the week. On Sunday night, get your backpack, textbooks, and notebooks ready, select the clothes you're going to wear, and set an alarm for getting up on time. Allocate sufficient time to avoid rushing. Don't leave home without

praying by yourself when you get up and with one of your parents before you leave for school.

4. Be extremely judicious in selecting your friends. We're often the average of the five friends we associate with most. When making friends, among many questions, ask yourself:

   o Am I honoring God and my parents or guardians?
   o Are my friends well-wishers?
   o Are they fair-weather friends?
   o Am I balancing my life properly?
   o Do we have compatibility in our beliefs and values?

5. Eliminate, or at least drastically minimize, any activity that does not help you achieve your academic goals. Personal time spent on social media and TV can be detrimental to your spiritual, intellectual, and physical growth. They can be addictive and cut into studying time and time with family, relatives, and friends.

6. When possible, sit in the front row of your classes, listen carefully to your teachers, and take excellent notes. It is easier to remember what you write than what you hear. You remember only 10 percent when you hear, but you'll remember at least 50 percent when you write.

7. Be nice to everyone. Don't pick fights. Being friendly with everyone does not mean everyone is a "close friend." In fact, having two or three very close friends is far better than have ten so-called friends.

8. Be competitive but not proud. Be competitive but compassionate. Raise the bar of excellence in everything you do—without making your team feel inferior to you. Everyone is ignorant of something; learn from everyone and genuinely appreciate their unique talents.

9. Learn teamwork because the real world requires solving problems in teams. Don't think you're better than anyone else. God created everyone with certain talents, and what

others have, you may not, and what you have, they may not. Be humble. It's a godly virtue.

For the In-Laws

Many people do not consider the fact that a person is marrying more than just their sweetheart. Marriage carries the positive and negative influences of mothers-in-law, fathers-in-law, brothers-in-law, and sisters-in-law. A common stereotype depicts a mother-in-law as an annoying intruder who thinks her son is never at fault and nothing can be done right by her daughter-in-law.

In any marriage, it takes time for a young couple to get into the groove of marital responsibilities. During that initial adjustment period, particularly in the first one or two years, the relational dynamics get complex, particularly if the in-laws exert their opinions unnecessarily. Misperceptions, misunderstandings, and marital arguments can get out of control if these dynamics are not understood. It's necessary for expectations to be clearly defined or made known early in the marriage. Generally, after the first child is born, the in-laws become a support mechanism as grandparents, granduncles, and grandaunts. It's amazing to watch the couples appreciate the positive influence of the in-laws on their first child. Giving time, being patient, and having good relationships with in-laws can help create a harmonious and joyful family.

The Bible features examples of good relationships with in-laws.

Ruth was very caring with her mother-in-law, Naomi, when the latter urged Ruth and her sister-in-law to stay in their homeland and remarry after her two sons and her husband died in Moab. Ruth insisted on going with Naomi to her homeland (Judah), and her classic response to Ruth is often repeated at weddings:

> Entreat me not to leave you. Or to turn back from following you; For wherever you go, I will go. And wherever you lodge, I will lodge; your people shall be

my people. And your God, my God. Where you die, I will die, and there will I be buried. The Lord do so to me, and more also. If anything, but death, parts you and me. (Ruth 1:16–17)

Eventually, Ruth found favor in Naomi's kinsman Boaz. His grandson was King David, and through his genealogy, Jesus Christ the Messiah came. This is a classic example of the loving bond between a daughter-in-law and a mother-in-law. One should admire Ruth's commitment to her family by marriage and Naomi's unselfish request of her daughters-in-law to stay behind and find husbands in their own homeland. This is a perfect example of unselfish love.

Peter attended to his mother-in-law when Jesus visited his home. When Jesus "touched her hand, the fever left her. And she arose and served them" (Matthew 8:15).

Moses respected his father-in-law's advice to delegate. Jethro told Moses:

> And you shall teach them the statutes and the law. (Exodus 18:20–22)

> Then it will be that every great matter they shall bring to you, but every small matter they themselves shall judge. So, it is easier for you, for they will bear the burden with you. (Exodus 18:22)

> So, Moses heeded the voice of his father-in-law and did all that he had said. (Exodus 18:24).

Some general principles for in-laws can help families function better:

1. Remember to give emotional space for the daughter-in-law to adjust. Don't encroach on the young couple's authorities or responsibilities. Go very slow until you develop a good understanding.

2. If your only child—your son— married a woman he loves, do not be possessive of your son's affection. That only leads to your daughter-in-law's alienation from you because she wants to know and feel that she's loved more by her husband than her husband loving his mother. As the husband, you must clarify to your wife that your love for her is special—and very different from your love for your mother. Clarify to your wife that spending time with your mother does not mean you love your wife any less. Clarify to your mother that you need to spend considerably more time with your new bride as you must learn of her likes and dislikes—and that you need to do mutually interesting things.

3. Communicate your good intent with your daughter-in-law or son-in-law before you appear to take matters into your own hands.

4. Draw the boundaries of understanding in the beginning stages of marriage so that there will not be major gaps in understanding.

5. Pray daily for your daughter-in-law or son-in-law. Seek God's wisdom in dealing with them lovingly and respectfully.

6. The young couple should respect their in-laws and afford them the dignity due to them. Try to win them over with loving intent.

Three Actions I Can Take for One Month after Reading This Chapter

1.

2.

3.

Chapter Twelve

COPING WITH DIFFERENT STAGES OF LIFE

Do not remember the former things, nor consider the
things of old. Behold, I will do a new thing, now it shall
spring forth; Shall you not know it? I will even make
a road in the wilderness and rivers in the desert.

—ISAIAH 43:18−19

L ife is dynamic, and we go through many stages. Different
stages call for different adjustments.

Parents as Newly Marrieds

Some couples are not fortunate to have children. Barrenness is very
emotionally difficult for a wife. Elkanah's wife, Hannah, was an
example. She was in bitterness of soul and prayed to the Lord and
wept in anguish (1 Samuel 1:10), but she overcame the problem by
turning to God for a miracle:

> If You will give your maidservant a male child, then I
> will give him to the Lord all the days of his life, and
> no razor shall come upon his head. (1 Samuel 1:11)

Eli, the priest, hears her prayer and tells her that God will grant her petition. Samuel was the first child born to Hannah and Elkanah "because the Lord remembered her" (1 Samuel 1:19). And Samuel becomes the first prophet and judge of Israel. Hannah was blessed with four sons and two daughters.

Clearly, Hannah's barrenness was for God's glory. She kept her vow to God by dedicating Samuel to the Lord's work with Eli. At least six examples exist in the Bible about barrenness of women. Two of these are famous: Sarah, Abraham's wife (Genesis 11:30), and Elizabeth, Zachariah's wife (Luke 1:7). In addition, Rebekah (Isaac's wife), Rachel (Jacob's younger wife), the anonymous wife of Manoah, the mother of Samson (Judges 13), and the "great woman" of Shunem, called the Shunammite (2 Kings 4:8–37).

Adoption

Today, more commonly than ever, couples adopt children not necessarily because of barrenness, but to help give a good, loving home for children who otherwise wouldn't have a safe, secure, and loving home. Some of our family friends adopted beautiful children apart from being blessed with their own biological children.

Firstborn

For all couples, especially young ones, the birth of the first child is such an exciting, anticipated event. We plan quite a bit for the first baby since there are so many unknowns, and everything is a first-time experience.

Dedication

In many churches, infant children are dedicated by pastors. Usually, in Baptist churches, a Bible is gifted in the dedication ceremony.

In the many stages of infants' growth, the young couple spends quality time with them—taking them for walks in a stroller, chasing after them when they're toddlers, playing with them in the preschool years, and simply enjoying them. Attending children's music recitals and going to sporting events puts pressure on one or both parents, but they manage to do all these things joyfully. Life seems "Rollie Polly" until the adolescent years.

Parents with Teenage Children

Many hormonal changes begin during adolescence. Boys and girls are growing up to assert themselves as they transition into young men and young women. They are neither fully children nor fully adults. Many self-identity challenges confront adolescents. The parents are also a bit confused with the physical and emotional changes of their young ones, and they must adapt with sensitivity, understanding, and love. Rash reactions on parents' parts can create unnecessary emotional stress for their children. School performance can begin to deteriorate or fluctuate, friendships unapproved by parents begin to form, and self-destructive habits begin to surface. Rebellious behavior can begin to manifest. Almost all parents face this tough stage of life with their teenagers.

The Bible has a few examples of well-behaved teenagers. Joseph, the eleventh son of Jacob (the grandson of Abraham), was shown favoritism by his father. His eleven brothers were envious of his colorful coat. Joseph shared a dream he had, which infuriated his brothers and his father (Genesis 37:1–11). The brothers sold Joseph to Midianites, and they brought him to Egypt. Joseph's fear of God made him the number two man in Egypt. God used Joseph to provide for his father and brothers and their families during a famine. He forgave his brothers and said, "But as for you, you meant evil against me; but God meant it for good, in order to bring it about it is this day, to save many people alive" (Genesis 50:20).

Every parent would love to have teenagers like Joseph or Daniel.

Daniel was taken as a captive by King Nebuchadnezzar in 605 BC. Daniel and his friends, Shadrach, Meshach, and Abednego, were asked by the king to eat a daily provision of king's delicacies and drink the wine he drank. After three years of training, they were going to serve the king:

> But Daniel purposed in his heart that he would not defile himself. (Daniel 1:8)

Daniel served four kings and lived a fruitful life of almost eighty-five years.

In the examples of Joseph and Daniel, we see that their goal to please God first resulted in them becoming the second most powerful persons in Egypt and Babylon.

Parents can benefit from a few principles that help their teenagers reach their full potential:

1. Teach them about God from the very start of their lives.
2. Love them without favoritism.
3. Do not be harsh in correcting them. Correct them lovingly.
4. Prevent them from pursuing wild and worldly pleasures at an immature age.
5. Do not condemn them for everything they do.

I recommend two excellent books for a detailed understanding of teenagers. Dr. Gary Chapman's *The Five Love Languages of Teenagers* teaches parents to talk the love languages of teens, and Dr. James Burns's *Understanding Your Teen: Shaping their Character, Facing their Realities* explains how parents must treat teens so they become responsible adults and what to do about common teen issues.

Parents at College Send-Offs

Settling in first-time college-bound children are bittersweet. As parents, you're excited that your child is going to college. It is a new phase of life. On the other hand, you might have concerns about your child going into unchartered territory. Apprehensive thoughts may run across your mind. How do you manage this happy-sad transition?

The Nine Do's

1. Submit the entire matter to God's hands. He's the One who planned your youngster's life even before their birth. He loves your children more than you can as parents. He created them, and He knew them before they were conceived (Psalm 139:13–16).
2. Prepare a checklist for all the tasks in settling your child, prioritize them, and accomplish the tasks in order. This will lessen the physical, emotional, and financial stress.
3. Infuse confidence in your child, especially if they are nervous by nature. You, as a parent, must be calm first.
4. Explain that you are trusting God to lead your child through their years of higher education.
5. Reinforce your family values without tiring out your child.
6. Communicate frequently with your youngster during their first semester, but do not conflict with their lectures, group projects, and other academic matters. Trust them fully.
7. Give your child the emotional space to strike a balance between your expectations of high academic performance and the freedom to explore their emotional needs.
8. One of the most common concerns of parents is addictive habits like excessive entertainment, social media, alcoholism, and drugs. Regular prayers, affirmations, and communications can help minimize them.

9. Higher educational institutions are places for "free-wheeling intellect." Let your child attend a good, Bible-teaching church where their values will not turn radical. The Holy Spirit will temper their radical ideas by helping them stay between the spiritual guardrails.

Walking-the-Aisle Time

One of the most exciting times for parents is seeing their graduates get a job, save money, get married, and raise a family. This is the time for dreams to come true for your child—and for the parents.

When the time came for Isaac to get a wife, his father, Abraham, planned an arranged marriage (Genesis 24). Samson ("man of the sun") was the last of the judges for the Israelites. His mother was barren, but she was visited by an angel of the Lord and told that she would have a son. He "shall be a Nazarite to God from the womb" (Judges 13:5).

Samson chose his wife from the Philistines and not from his own people of Israel (Judges 14:1). He was deceived by his father-in-law, and then he went and married a woman he loved, Delilah. Violating the Nazarene tradition, he allowed Delilah to know the secret of his strength in his hair, and the Philistines captured him. While he was tied between two pillars in the temple of Dagon, he asked God to restore his strength for one last act. He braced himself against the pillars and pushed with all his might. The temple collapsed, and many Philistines died–and Samson did too.

No parent has total control of who their dear daughter or son marries or how they decide to marry—whether through an arranged marriage or by allowing them to fall in love with each other. Parents must walk a tightrope when their son or daughter marries against their will, liking, or blessing. Only God can grant you the peace and calm in such a scenario. You cannot afford to anger your child to the point of having no further relationship with them. It's best to put this matter in God's hands. He has a way of bringing something good even from what seems like a bad choice on your child's part: "All things work together for good to them that love God, and to those who are called according to His purpose" (Romans 8:28).

I have seen the bitterest relationships between parents and children who married against their will patched up once the first baby arrives. The grandparents suddenly see themselves in that baby and start loving that grandchild immediately. Very soon, the days of ill will are gone.

When your son or daughter is getting married, a few principles can help make the wedding experience a pleasant one for everyone:

1. Having trusted the Lord completely, demonstrate your spiritual anchor in Him and do not be perturbed by any deviations (small or big) from your plans or the groom's and bride's plans. Impatience creates disharmony, which snowballs through the entire wedding process.
2. Be in a state of prayer for the whole wedding function to go smoothly and joyously. It's as important, if not more, for your dear one's marriage. A wedding is usually a one-day event, but marriage is a lifetime commitment.
3. If your son or daughter violates the values you taught them during their pre-wedding celebrations, just pray and pray and pray. The Lord will ease your anxieties.

Parents become empty nesters once their children are married and have their own families. This can be a difficult transition. Dr. Jim Burns's *Finding Joy in the Empty Nest: Discover Purpose and Passion in the Next Phase of Life* gives a detailed treatment of this topic.

Grandchildren

It's so exciting to hear that you will be grandparents soon. We can't wait for the actual moment of arrival of the grand.

Beware of the way you comment on your grandchild on your

first hospital visit. Please don't say that the baby looks like someone on your side of the family. That is sure to start the admiration the wrong way.

It's natural that grandparents will be talking about the baby for much of the day; in fact, sharing the great news about your grandchild may receive subdued response if you overdo it. Most likely, the wallpaper on your smartphone will be your grandchild's picture. That's all right. I did it too. If you show too much enthusiasm while flashing that picture to everybody you run into, it can become boring. "Children's children are a crown to the aged, and parents are the pride of their children" (Proverbs 17:6).

Principles for Raising Grandchildren

1. Love your grandchildren and avoid repeating the mistakes you made while you were raising your children. Bless them all the time. Joseph's father, Jacob, said, "Bring them to me, please, that I may bless them" (Genesis 48:9).

2. Love your grands unconditionally. Laban, Jacob's father-in-law, "kissed his grandchildren and his daughter and blessed them" (Genesis 31:55).

3. Don't show any favoritism to any of your grandchildren. Even when they are tiny, they can sense your partiality. The impression in their hearts can be negative. "If you show partiality, you commit sin" (James 2:9).

4. Reward your grandchildren when they show positive behaviors in the important areas of their lives:

   o academic excellence
   o carefully chosen friends
   o hygiene
   o manners and etiquette
   o physical fitness
   o spiritual values and growth

- o sportsmanship
- o work ethic in chores

5. Create savings accounts for college and get life insurance: "A good person leaves an inheritance for their children's children" (Proverbs 13:22).

6. Tell lots of stories to your grands and embed good morals in them. Adults remember their grandparents' stories, and the values imparted in them. Lois was the grandmother, and Eunice was the mother of Timothy, Paul's young protégé. Eunice, a Jewish believer, was married to a Greek man (Acts 16:1). Lois was either Eunice's mother or mother-in-law. It's likely that Timothy's father died when he was young. Perhaps that's why we see Paul taking on a fatherly role with Timothy. Paul often refers to Timothy as "my true son in the faith" (1 Corinthians 4:17; 1 Timothy 1:2, 18). Lois and Eunice must have raised Timothy, according to the scriptures. Paul recognized these women's positive influences on Timothy, and he became Paul's travel companion in his ministry (Romans 16:21). Eventually, the influence of Paul as a "guardian" resulted in Timothy becoming a very young pastor at the church in Ephesus. My grandmother, Flossie, had a very positive influence in all the above-mentioned areas on my sister and me until our teen years when she went to be with the Lord.

7. Grandparents are told by God to make the things that your eyes have seen "known to your children and your children's children" (Deuteronomy 4:9).

8. Grandchildren have their own responsibilities toward their grandparents. Grandchildren must love and honor their parents and their grandparents. Grandparents are an important part of the family teaching. Therefore, grandchildren must actively listen to their grandparents and glean their expert knowledge and experiential wisdom from them. "Gray hair is a crown of splendor; it is attained in the way of righteousness" (Proverbs

16:31). This will prevent grandchildren from committing mistakes and spare them from unnecessary agony. Taking care of grandparents is an expected quality in today's world. It's a blessing for them: "Do not cast me off in the times of old age; do not forsake me when my strength fails" (Psalm 71:9).

9. Grandparents can teach faithfulness to God via their life experiences. King David said, "I have been young, and now am old; yet I have not seen the righteous forsaken nor his descendants begging bread" (Psalm 37:25).

Today, grandparents are living longer and healthier lives: "They shall still bear fruit in old age; they shall be fresh and flourishing" (Psalm 92:14).

There are bad and good examples of grandparents in the Bible. Athaliah, the mother of King Ahaziah of Judah, was a bad example. Upon Ahaziah's death, she had the royal family killed so she alone could reign. But Jehosheba, one of Ahaziah's sisters, hid her son Joash. During Athaliah's six-year reign, her grandson and nurse hid in the temple, and when Joash was seven years old, the high priest anointed him publicly and declared him Judah's king. When Athaliah was furious, the high priest had her executed—and Joash ruled Judah for forty years (2 Kings 11).

Ruth, Naomi's daughter-in-law from Moab, was an excellent example of being a loyal, faithful daughter-in-law to Naomi. She was a wonderful wife to Boaz, a good mother to Obed, and a good grandmother to Jesse. Her great grandson, David, is still considered the greatest king of Israel.

Grandparenting is a generational responsibility: "One generation shall praise Your works to another and shall declare Your mighty acts" (Psalm 145:4). Moses tells the assembly of Israel: "Remember the days of old, consider the years of many generations. Ask your father, and he will show you, your elders, and they will tell you" (Deuteronomy 32:7).

Children, grandchildren, and grandparents form a symbiotic relationship in a family. When all people consider that relationship to be God's designed blessing, we'll have more harmonious, productive, and responsible family members and valuable citizens.

Spousal Separation and/or Divorce

Coping with separation and/or divorce can be a traumatic experience. Much is written about the subject in the fields of psychology, sociology, and religion. What does the Bible say?

> And I say to you, whoever divorces his wife, except for sexual immorality, and marries another, commits adultery; and whoever marries her who is divorced commits adultery. (Matthew 19:9)

In the rest of Matthew 19, Jesus answers the questions related to divorce.

The apostle Paul also addresses marital separation:

> But if the unbeliever departs, let him depart; a brother or a sister is not under bondage in such cases. But God has called us to peace. (1 Corinthians 7:15)

Paul has more to say in 1 Corinthians 7:15 by addressing the unmarried and the widows. God sent a warning through the writer of Hebrews:

> Marriage is honorable among all, and the bed undefiled; but fornicators and adulterers God will judge. (Hebrews 13:4)

Some marriages end in separation or divorce because a Christian believer marries a nonbeliever. The apostle Paul also sent a warning:

> Do not be unequally yoked together with unbelievers. For what fellowship has righteousness with

lawlessness? And what communion has light with darkness? (2 Corinthians 6:14)

Husbands, likewise, dwell with them with understanding, giving honor to the wife, as to the weaker vessel, and as being heirs together to the grace of life, that your prayers may not be hindered. (1 Peter 3:7)

Husbands, love your wives, just as Christ also loved the church and gave Himself for her. (Ephesians 5:25)

In the area of physical intimacy, marriages can be lacking because of emotional separation or alienation, money matters, lack of fairness, or a host of other reasons. Paul gave advice for the case of occasional abstinence from physical intimacy between husband and wife:

Do not deprive one another except with consent for a time, that you may give yourselves to fasting and prayer; and come together again so that Satan does not tempt you because of your lack of self-control. (1 Corinthians 7:5)

Prevention is better than cure. Following God's principles and advice helps Christian couples avoid separation and divorce. God created you as husband and wife and brought you into holy union, and He does not want you to separate or divorce. Christian counseling is available in many ways, including pastors and elders in the church and elders in the family.

Commitment to the institution of marriage according to the biblical ideas is the ultimate solution. All other approaches are usually suboptimal; they're temporal paths that end in the breakup of a marriage rather than putting it back together.

As a couple, when one or both of you are unhappy in your marriage, your children are the first ones to experience the emotional pain or even physical pain and dysfunctional academics, careers, or marriages. Broken marriages spread the negativity across society.

Death of a Loved One: Expected or Unexpected

Physical death can be expected or unexpected. The trauma faced by a family varies depending upon which one it is facing.

Examples of expected death include old age and prolonged illnesses like cancer, dementia, or Alzheimer's.

Examples of unexpected death include heart attacks, accidents, suicides, murders, and natural disasters (earthquakes, tsunamis, hurricanes, and tornados).

In the Bible, we see examples of both types of deaths. Abel, the second son of Adam and Eve, was murdered by his own brother. This was the first unexpected death for the first parents (Genesis 4:1). We don't know how devastating it must've been for them to experience this tragedy—let alone for God Himself—to see such a horrible act due to jealousy. Fortunately, God blessed Adam and Eve with another son, Seth: "For God has appointed another seed for me instead of Abel, whom Cain killed" (Genesis 4:25).

Adam died an expected death at the ripe old age of 930 years (Genesis 5:5). Seth died naturally after a blessed 912 years (Genesis 5:8).

When the sons of God took women for wives, there were giants on the earth. The Lord saw that the wickedness of man was great on the earth and that every intent in his heart was only evil continually.

God "was sorry that He had made man—and was grieved in His heart" (Genesis 6:2–6). God chose Noah and his small family to be spared from His wrath, through the Great Flood, which prevailed for 150 days (Genesis 6:7–10:32).

The patriarchs who descended from Noah included Abraham and his sons Isaac, Ishmael, and Jacob who was called Israel by God (Genesis 11–50).

King David of Israel had a devastating emotional breakdown

when his very handsome son was killed by Joab, David's commander, and ten young men struck and killed Absalom (2 Samuel 18:14–19:8). We can't imagine when parents languish for a child who is killed in a murder, war, explosion, or accident. When families face such unexpected and shocking deaths in their lives, how can they handle it? Fortunately, Christian families have a reasonably good support mechanism available at such times—with pastors, Bible study groups, Christian families and friends, and counselors.

At times like this, parents must rely on complete surrender to God's grace. Though it's common and natural to dislike God at such times, we must recognize that the devil, our enemy, is always ready to discourage us, mock our faith in God, and turn us away from following Him. If we stick to our unfluctuating faith in God, we'll make it through the valley. Tragedies like these involve different emotions: denial and grief (phase 1), indifference (phase 2), and acceptance (phase 3). Phase 1 can last a few months to a few years, phase 2 can be shorter, and phase 3, though relatively short after Phase 2, can last until we see our children in heaven with Jesus.

Fathers process denial and grief much differently than their wives do. Women grieve by talking about the tragedy with their families, friends, and church folks. They're networkers by nature, and they have a decent emotional support system. Fathers, as men, tend to stay away from emotions and are hesitant to share with their close family and friends.

Intense events, like the sudden death of a child, create very stressful emotions, including depression, withdrawal, addictions, and divorce. Relying on Jesus is the only solution for any parent to cope with the sudden death of a dear one. Romans 8:28 is always true, and after a few years, we see how the gracious hand of God was architecting events in our lives to make us stronger in our dependence upon Him as our ultimate source of comfort, strength, and future plans to bring Him glory.

Important Disclaimer

Many suggestions have been made in this chapter, most of which are based on my personal experiences over seventy-four years. However, you are strongly recommended to consult professional Christian counselors, pastors, and others who have been trained and are experienced in these matters. My principles are for guiding the reader rather than dogmatically prescribing solutions. Also, my suggestions are from a very deep and unwavering faith and trust in God. If your faith level in Him is relatively low, seek guidance from a professional counselor.

Three Actions I Can Take for One Month after Reading This Chapter

1.
2.
3.

ABOUT THE AUTHOR

Dr. David J. Sumanth has been an internationally published author and editor for forty-four years, with McGraw-Hill, Elsevier, St. Lucie Press, CRC Press, Taylor and Francis, IIE Press, Inderscience, and MCB University Press. He pioneered formal "productivity engineering" education in 1979 at the University of Miami (the U) where he has been a professor emeritus of industrial engineering since 2007. For fifty-four years, his industry experience, teaching, research, and consulting covered the areas of "Customer Delight Management," Engineering Management, Management of Technology and Innovation, Industrial Engineering, Productivity and Quality Management, Reengineering, "3-D Poverty," Strategic Planning, and Total Productivity Management. His degrees include BE (Distinction) and ME (Distinction) in Mechanical Engineering from Osmania University in India and an MS and a PhD in Industrial Engineering from Illinois Institute of Technology (IIT or Illinois Tech) in Chicago. David's honors include Who's Who in Science and Engineering, Who's Who in American Education, Who's Who in America, Who's Who in the World, and 5000 Personalities of the World. His recognitions include Outstanding Industrial Engineer of the Year, George Washington Honor Medal for Excellence in

Economic Education, Fellow of the World Academy of Productivity Science, The Alexander Orr Award for Teaching Excellence at "the U," Iron Arrow (the highest honor at "the U"), Albert Nelson Marquis Lifetime Achievement Award, and Marquis Distinguished Humanitarian Award. David served nine years as the founding chief judge of Florida Sterling Award for Quality and is a member of the Heritage Society of "the U." He holds several distinguished professorships internationally.

David's insights in this book are drawn from his fifty-plus years of university teaching, research, consulting, public speaking, and face-to-face interactions with hundreds of thousands of people, including CEOs, executives, presidents, prime ministers, government leaders, and church leaders and families in more than one hundred countries. David's powerful public speaking talent, conversational teaching and writing styles, caring passion for people, and tough love have made him a "humanity-builder." His unique approach with people has transcended cultures and has resulted in "zero-failure people" in companies, governments, classrooms, and churches.

David has been a licensed minister for nineteen years at Christ Journey Church in Florida and honorary executive pastor for seventeen years at CPF/Elim Church in India. He has been a bible study teacher for sixty-three years, including fourteen at Wesley Church in India; five in Mount Carmel Baptist Church, twenty-nine at Christ Journey Church in Florida, and fifteen at Wayside Baptist Church.

David and Chaya, his bride of forty-nine years, have had two sons. Dr. John J. Sumanth, associate professor at Wake Forest University, is married to Jaya, and they have two daughters: Miah and Anna. Paul has been in heaven since his twentieth year.

David and Chaya Sumanth founded the Paul J. Sumanth Ministries, Inc. (www.pjsm.org) in 2001. Since his early retirement in 2007, David has been leading the educational efforts for destitute children in India. Starting with sixty children and one campus in 2001, it has expanded to fifteen campuses and two thousand children by God's grace and has graduated more than twenty thousand children from the tenth grade. Many have earned engineering and MBA degrees. David has also trained more than five thousand pastors and church leaders in the United States, India, Colombia, and Honduras. Chaya's and David's parents are with the Lord. David's sister, Vivian, and Chaya's sister, Sulochana, and their families live in India.

Printed in the United States
by Baker & Taylor Publisher Services